CONTENTS

SECTION EIGHT: MIDDLE SCHOOL URBAN LEGENDS

SECTION NINE: CAMPUS KINDNESS

SECTION TEN: MISCELLANEOUS SURVIVAL TIPS

INTRODUCTION

See this really dorky picture right here? That's me, Marko, when I was in middle school. Nice shirt collar, huh? Can you tell I wasn't the most popular kid in school? Uh, yeah.

How about this groovy picture? That's me, Kurt, back during my middle school years. That haircut *rocked*, huh? Sure, whatever.

We wanted you to see those pictures—as embarrassing as they are—because we want you to know that we remember what it's like to be a middle school student. Partly, we remember because we've been working with middle schoolers in churches for a long time. We don't work with high school kids or with any other age group. That's because we're both convinced of a few things:

- First, middle schoolers are the coolest people in the world. Really! We'd rather hang out with a group of middle school students than any other age group.

- Next, God really cares (we mean, *REALLY CARES*) about middle school students—about you. And we believe God is stoked about the possibility of having a close relationship with you.

- Finally, the middle school years (from about 11 to 14 years old) are HUGELY important in building a FAITH that will last for your whole life.

This book is the fourth in a new series: The Middle School Survival Series. The first book is all about your faith (that's why it's called *My Faith*—duh!). The second book is about your Family (it's called, not-so-surprisingly, *My Family*). The third book is also available now—it's called *My Friends*. And we have two more books planned for the series: *My Changes* and *My Future*. We hope you'll read them all!

Oh, one more thing: you don't have to read these 75 "chapters" in any particular order. It's not that kind of book. You *can* read them in order if you want (if you're one of those people who likes order!); or you can just flip through and read whatever catches your attention.

We believe in you, and we'll be praying for you (really, we will), that while you read this, you'll grow in your understanding of God (just like the Bible says Jesus did when he was your age!), of how much God loves you, and of how God would do anything to let you know him!

Kurt and Marko

SECTION 1
MIDDLE SCHOOL
BASICS

WHOSE IDEA *WAS* SCHOOL, ANYWAY?

Well, there's no one answer to that one. In some ways, you could say it was God's idea because God instructed parents to teach and guide their kids. And that process of teaching and guiding shifted over the years.

One of the earliest groups of people to have an educational system (a school system) for *all* kids (not just the rich ones) was the Jewish people. All Jewish kids (well, all boys—only some of the girls), no matter if they were rich or poor, went to study with a rabbi (say RAB-bye). Rabbis are Jewish leaders, so it'd be like if you went to study with the pastor of your church.

And get this—Jewish kids memorized the entire Torah (say TOR-ruh)—the first five books of our Bible: Genesis, Exodus, Leviticus, Numbers, and Deuteronomy. Seriously! Can you imagine trying to memorize that much? Grab a Bible, flip through those pages, and check 'em out.

The kids in the Jewish schools didn't just memorize stuff, though. They also had long conversations about what the stories and teachings meant. By the time they were 12 years old, they could quote the entire Torah and answer all kinds of complicated questions about Jewish beliefs. How does that make you feel about *your* homework?

Anyhow, except for the Jewish people and a few other exceptions, for thousands of years schools were for rich kids only. But about 100 to 150 years ago, people in many countries of the world decided *everyone* has the right to an education. Even then, until much more recently, school was offered through only the eighth grade for most kids.

Sometimes the idea that "school is good for you" might feel like a parent trying to get you to eat Brussels sprouts. But really, whether or not you like all your classes, you know it's true. No matter if you want to be a doctor or a factory worker, a mom or an artist, going to school is a process that helps you learn to think, and it'll help you no matter who you are or what you become.

WHY LEARNING IS A GOOD THING

Take a few seconds to think about some of the stuff you've learned. You've learned to walk and talk and throw a ball. You've learned to load and unload the dishwasher. You've learned the difference between a noun and a verb. You've learned how to surf the Web and how to send an attachment in an e-mail. The fact that you're now holding this book in your hands is proof you've learned how to read.

Now take a few seconds to think about what your life would be like if you didn't know how to do the stuff we just listed. Kinda weird, huh? The truth is all of us are learning stuff all the time. One place we learn is in the school of life. All of us—grown-ups, too—are enrolled there. So there's a whole bunch of stuff you've learned just because you're experiencing the joys of being alive. You've learned most of it naturally, and you probably can't remember exactly how or when you learned it.

Another place we all learn is in the school of—well, the school of school! It's in the school of school that we learn some of the more formal stuff like reading, writing, and arithmetic.

So here's some bad news: Like it or not, you're *always* in school.

Here's some good news: Because you're always in school, you're almost always learning. And learning is a really good thing. Maybe you need to hear that one more time: Learning is a really good thing! In the Bible it says, "Intelligent people are always ready to learn. Their ears are open for knowledge" (Proverbs 18:15, New Living Translation).

For some of you, learning comes easily. For others, learning to be a learner is going to be a learning process. (Huh?) We know you could be doing lots of other stuff right now, like playing video games, duct-taping your little brother to the wall, or trying to discover if cats really do always land on their feet. Instead, you're reading this book. And the fact that you're reading this book means you're a learner, and learning is a really good thing.

Go ahead—pat yourself on the back.

DID JESUS GO TO SCHOOL?

Jesus totally went to school. Isn't that a riot? It's hard to think of him sitting in the fourth row, right behind some little know-it-all, just to the left of that kid who's always picking his nose, and in front of the student who falls asleep in class all the time.

We know Jesus went to school because *all* Jewish kids (all boys, that is, and some girls) went to school. They studied with a rabbi (see the previous chapter) and learned *tons* of stuff. Most kids also studied a "trade" (a skill that would be used for a job someday), and they usually learned this from their parents. So Jesus would have gone to school for part of the day, and then studied carpentry with his dad—Joseph—the rest of the day.

Here's an interesting thing to think about: We don't really know what Jesus knew about himself and at what age. Like, the Bible makes it clear that Jesus was completely human and completely God. (That's 200 percent, which can make your brain hurt if you think about it too much.) Yet the Bible also makes it clear Jesus grew up like a normal kid. Check out this verse:

AND JESUS GREW IN WISDOM AND STATURE, AND IN FAVOR WITH GOD AND MEN. (LUKE 2:52)

Sure, the verse doesn't say, "Jesus went to school, and got pretty good grades." But what it *does* tell us is that Jesus grew up. Okay, we know you're thinking, *Duh!* And you're wondering if you can keep reading this book because we, the authors, must be the two stupidest guys ever to write something so obvious as though it were important. But wait—it *is* important. Jesus didn't just grow up physically (that's what the verse means when it says he grew in "stature"). Jesus also grew "in wisdom"—ooh, that's the key phrase!

When the Bible says Jesus "grew in wisdom," it means he became wiser and smarter, right? That also means he didn't know *everything* since the moment he was born (super-baby!). Now, we don't know exactly when Jesus understood he was the Son of God, the Messiah sent to save the world. Although he seems to understand it by the time he's about 12 years old because he says some stuff to his parents after they lost him on a trip to Jerusalem that makes it pretty clear *he knows.* (You can read about it in Luke 2:41-52. The verse in the middle of the previous page is the last verse of that story.)

All of this to say: YES! Jesus went to school! And he wasn't just sitting in class feeling bored because he had to listen to stuff he already knew (because he's God). Jesus actually learned, and he grew in wisdom. Just like you're doing (we hope!).

WHY DO WE NEED IT?

Did you read the last chapter ("Did Jesus Go to School?")? If you didn't, turn back and read it before you read this one.

Here's why we had you do that: We don't believe the best reason for providing a school is so you have to memorize history dates or learn long division. We believe the best reason for providing a school is to help you "grow in wisdom"—just like Jesus did when he was your age.

Wisdom, you might know, is different than being smart. Being *smart* is about knowing lots of stuff. *Wisdom* means knowing how to make good decisions with the stuff you know. Knowing it's not a good idea to skateboard at night into oncoming freeway traffic—that's smart. But you could know that and still make the unwise choice of doing it.

Ooh—we want to tell you a little about your brain. Really, this is cool stuff—so stop pretending you're bored. Here's the deal: Just before your young teenage years—like, when you were 9 and 10 years old—your brain did something wild. It grew millions (seriously!) of extra connections (called "synapses") between different parts of your brain. These millions of extra (brand new!) connections meant that you had to think in new ways because your brain was working better now. It's kind of like getting an upgrade on a computer system.

And now that you're a young teenager, something equally wild is happening in your brain: Some of those new connections are dying off. Ha!

No, really. For some reason, God invented our brains to do this. And the truly wild thing is that the extra connections that die off (they actually disintegrate and go away forever) are the ones that don't get used. You get to keep only the connections you use.

What that means is this: How you use your brain during your young teenage years will impact the rest of your life. If for the next two years you did nothing but jump rope and say "jump rope" over and over and over again, then your brain would get really, really good at thinking about jumping rope. But your brain wouldn't get very good at, say, math or thinking about God or understanding words on a page.

Are you seeing where we're going? School is important because it helps you think in new and different ways. It helps you exercise the brain God created for you. And when you exercise your brain like that—especially during your young teenage years—it will serve you well for the rest of your life. Yeehaw!

SO MANY CLASSES, SO LITTLE TIME

Do you ever feel like you've just gotten started in one class, when suddenly the bell rings (or the buzzer sounds or whatever signal you have at your school that tells you class is over), and it's time to go to the next class? Or if you don't change classes and teachers at your school, do you ever think it's weird how often you move from subject to subject?

Our experience is that some students love this kind of variety, but it drives other students crazy. We've heard lots of students ask, "Why can't they let us stay in one class until we've finished a project?"

Now, we know we told you in the Introduction to this book that you're allowed to read the chapters in any order you want. And, really, you can. But the chapter before this one (that talks about how your brain is developing) would be really helpful here. Don't want to read it? Fine, be that way! Whatever—it's your book.

Let's see...before we started whining...oh, yeah.

At this stage in your life, it's *way* more important to get exposed to lots and lots of different subjects than to go super-deep in one or two subjects. You need to consider tons of ideas. (Okay, maybe not literally *tons* because that would be a big, heavy box full of ideas.) You need to hear about a crazy-wide variety of subjects: weights and measurements, the process of photosynthesis, the

Civil War, leverage, why mammals are warm-blooded, how the stomach works, the history of your own state, how to measure the side of a triangle, and so many more things.

Here are two oversimplified reasons for this variety:

1. It will help you start thinking about what subjects interest you the most. Then someday in the future (even in high school), you can start digging a bit deeper into those things.

2. It will help your brain work better. (Really, did you read the last chapter yet?) You'll become both smarter *and* wiser. Cool, huh?

So the next time you feel there are just too many subjects being covered in school, remind yourself that it's a way-cool opportunity for you and your brain.

WHY IS IT SO BORING?

It's true—school can be boring. We aren't going to try to convince you that going to school is the most exciting part about being alive. But there are *more* boring things. If you think school is boring, you should try watching paint dry or sitting through one of Kurt's Sunday school lessons—yikes!

There are all sorts of reasons why school can be boring, but we want to focus on the two biggies:

First, school can be boring because it's *school.* Think about it, a typical school day is six or seven hours spent listening to lectures, taking notes, and stressing about pop quizzes. School is listening to grown-ups talk about stuff you couldn't care less about and wondering if the person sitting next to you noticed the little puddle of drool you left on your desk when you dozed off. Sure, there can be moments of excitement, like a small explosion in the science lab. But other than that—school is BOOOOORRRRRIIIINNGG.

Second, school can be boring because you've decided to keep it that way. By now, you've already been in school for more than half your life. The same routine day in and day out, ever since you were five or six years old. So it's totally understandable that you've become bored with the routine. Most people do.

Allow us to get "parent-y and youth pastor-ly" on you for a second. We've learned (remember, learning is a good thing...) that lots of life's experiences are made better or worse by our attitudes.

You can't always decide *what* happens to you in life, but you can decide *how* you handle it. For now, you don't have the freedom to decide *if* you'll go to school, but you can decide *how* you'll go to school. In fact, that's the whole reason we wrote this book. We know going to school can be really boring and there's a lot about school you can't change. We also know that since you're going to be at school quite a bit over the next few years, it's probably worth thinking about how to make the most of it.

The rest of this book will help you do just that.

WILL I EVER USE THE STUFF I'M LEARNING?

Of course you'll use this stuff! Believe it or not, we use the stuff we learned in middle school almost every day. Kurt uses the stuff he learned in quantum physics, algebra, and the rocket science class he took in eighth grade to try to help the United States land on Mars. And Marko uses the stuff he learned in household education to make really yummy cookies. Um, that's not totally true. Kurt got a D- in algebra. But Marko does make really yummy cookies.

Look, we're not going to try to convince you of something you know isn't true. Obviously you won't use a lot of the stuff you're learning very often. We can't remember the last time somebody asked us when Christopher Columbus discovered America (1492, in case you're wondering) or the last time we reached for our algebra calculators. (Of course, if Kurt had reached for his once in a while, he might have bumped that grade up to a C.) But even though you won't use a lot of the stuff you learn every day, you'll be surprised at how often you'll find yourself reaching back into the caverns of your mind and pulling out stuff you need to know. It'll be old, dusty, rusty stuff that you haven't used in a while, but you'll be glad you have it! And when it happens it's actually kinda cool.

It's also kinda cool to think about the fact that God uses the stuff you're learning at school to help you learn more about how he wired you. Some of you actually like math because it comes naturally to you and you like messing around with numbers. Some of you like English because you like reading and writing. Some of you like P.E. because...well, because you're seventh-grade boys. Everybody has God-given gifts, abilities, and interests that God hopes we'll put to good use. If there's a class or two out of your entire day at school that you really like, it may be time to start thinking, *Hey, I like this class, and I'm pretty good at it. Maybe God has gifted me in this area.*

It doesn't happen all the time, but it's amazing how often we'll meet grown-ups whose careers have a whole lot to do with the subjects they really liked when they were in school.

"I'M GOING TO USE ALL THIS STUFF I'M LEARNING LATER? COME ON, LIKE I'M EVER GOING TO NEED TO KNOW HOW TO DISSECT A FROG."

—CHAD, 8TH GRADE

LEARNING ABOUT LIFE, NOT JUST ALGEBRA

You learn a lot at school, but it's important to remember that you're learning a whole lot more than reading, writing, and arithmetic (which, by the way, you *do* use every day). Being a middle school student teaches you all kinds of stuff that will make every day of the rest of your life a little better. Stuff like:

Self-discipline. Learning to finish an assignment on time, forcing yourself to listen to a boring lecture, and getting to class on time are little ways you're learning the important art of self-discipline.

Perseverance. *Perseverance* is just a big word for "never giving up." Refusing to give up in a tough class, working on an eight-week science project, and rewriting your English paper for the third time are little ways you're learning to hang in there.

Respect for authority. Aghhh! Did we have to include this one? Yes, we did. At school there are lots of people you need to respect—even when you don't feel like it. Life works pretty much the same way.

How to get along with others. This is one of life's most important skills. Let's say that one more time: Learning to get along with others is one of life's most important skills. Getting along with others is tough stuff. It doesn't mean you always do what people want. It doesn't mean you have to be best friends with everybody. It doesn't mean you always have to agree with everybody. Getting along with others simply means you learn how to be the young man or woman God has created you to be without being an idiot in the process. It sounds easy enough, but trust us—it's tougher than it sounds. You can also trust us when we say that going to school every day is a perfect place to figure it all out.

The value of friendship. You've probably already discovered how important it is to have a few of the right kinds of friends at school. Friends who will look out for you, stick up for you, believe in you, and never give up on you. School is helping you choose good friends, and it's helping you become a good friend. These are two skills you'll need for the rest of your life.

The art of being a Christian. If you go to a public school, it took you about two seconds on the first day of school to realize most of the kids you spend your day with don't have a relationship with Jesus. When do you speak up? When do you keep your mouth shut? How do you stay true to Jesus without looking like a goody-goody? Being a Christian when most of the people around you aren't isn't easy to do, but it's important. It's important because God's plan for reaching out to people who don't know him yet is to use the people who already do. And since you're reading this book, you're probably someone God wants to use at your school to let others in on his love for them.

SECTION 2
WHERE SCHOOL HAPPENS

WHY YOUR SCHOOL SETTING SHOULD INFLUENCE HOW YOU READ THIS BOOK

There are different kinds of schools, right? You know that. Take seventh grade as an example. Here are some of the variations we've seen:

- Public junior high where seventh grade is the youngest grade

- Public middle school where seventh grade is the middle grade

- Public middle school where seventh grade is the oldest grade

- Public school where seventh grade is the only grade (Really! A whole school of only seventh graders!)

- Public school that has kindergarten through eighth grade, so seventh grade is just about the oldest

- Public school that has junior high (or middle school) and high school combined

- Private Christian school versions of each of these

- Private school (not a Christian school) versions of all of these

- Home school where the student is never with other students

- Home school where the student is with other students either for part of every day, or for a few days each week

STUFF YOU MAY NOT HAVE LEARNED IN MIDDLE SCHOOL: DURING WORLD WAR II, IBM BUILT THE COMPUTERS THE NAZIS USED TO MANAGE THEIR DEATH/CONCENTRATION CAMPS.

- And so many more, like military schools, missionary kid boarding schools, international English-speaking schools, foreign-language immersion schools, and others.

There are so many different ways to attend school. And since you probably haven't experienced more than one of them (maybe two at the most), you might not think about the fact that what kind of school you attend will have a big impact on how you read this book.

For example, a chapter on picking your classes would be very different for a public school student than for a homeschooler. Or chapter 13 about the cafeteria lady—well, for the home school student, that's probably Mom.

As we write this book, we're trying to be aware of all these kinds of students, just like we're aware of them when we work in our middle school ministries. And we've written three specific chapters (following this one) for the three most common readers: public school students, Christian school students, and home school students. But we need you to help us out.

Here's our part: We'll try to remember that your school might be different than someone else's school. And we'll try to write in such a way as to include you in all the chapters.

Here's your part: We won't succeed at this all the time. So in some of the chapters, you might need to think about how what we're saying could be "translated" for your school situation.

Deal?

A SPECIAL CHAPTER FOR PUBLIC SCHOOL STUDENTS

There are wonderful benefits of attending a public school. One of the most important ones is realizing God calls all of us to live out our faith with and in front of people who aren't followers of Jesus. If you attend a public school, this opportunity is in your face all the time, every day.

You don't have to look very far for a chance to stand up for what you believe. And your faith will be tested and pushed and bumped into all the time—which is great for strengthening your faith.

You have a great opportunity to tell friends about Jesus—friends who might not know him. And you have a very cool opportunity to learn from people who believe differently than you do.

That's all very cool. But there are some challenges to attending a public school also.

It's a lot harder to stand up for what you believe in a public school. For instance, it's pretty easy for a student at a private Christian school to give an oral report about Jesus. But that takes some pretty major courage in a public school, doesn't it? It can be tempting, in a bad way, to really hide your faith in a public school.

We're all influenced by the people we spend time with, which can be a good thing or a bad thing. Public schools provide lots of opportunities for peer pressure to make lousy choices—choices that really aren't best for you in the long run.

If you go to a public school, it's important you're aware of both the good potential and the not-so-good potential that are both really normal in this situation. Talk about these with your parents, your closest friends, and your youth group. Talk about them with God, too.

Make a choice to "go for it" with the cool opportunities a public school offers you. And be extra cautious about the negative pressures you'll experience.

MY SCHOOL

A SPECIAL CHAPTER FOR CHRISTIAN SCHOOL STUDENTS

Lots of students who read this book attend private Christian schools. Kurt's middle school daughter attends a private Christian school. And we've both worked with thousands of Christian school kids over the years, spoken in dozens—if not hundreds—of Christian school chapels, and spent thousands of hours on the campuses of Christian schools. All those experiences tell us one thing: Not all Christian schools (or Christian school students) are the same!

You might find that your Christian school isn't all that different from a public school. You might find that the same issues public school kids face— the pressure to party and cheat and make all kinds of bad choices—are just as common at your school. If that's true, you might want to back up and read chapter 10, "A Special Chapter for Public School Students."

Or you might find that your Christian school is a wonderfully safe place where your faith in Jesus is greatly encouraged.

Either way, here are two things we've noticed that Christian school students should watch for:

Isolation from the world. Yeah, that's a big word and a big idea. Being *isolated* means to be totally cut off from something—like people living on an island are isolated from the mainland. We've seen so many Christian school kids who don't know anyone who *isn't* a Christian, and that's not a good thing. The Bible encourages us to be "in the world,"

STUFF YOU MAY NOT HAVE LEARNED IN MIDDLE SCHOOL: ERNEST VINCENT WRIGHT WROTE *GADSBY*, A NOVEL WITH MORE THAN 50,000 WORDS, NONE OF WHICH CONTAINS THE LETTER "E".

but "not of the world" (John 17:13-19; Romans 12:2). That means we should stay strong to who we are as followers of Jesus. But it also means we're to be connected, right here in the world. If you find yourself feeling isolated from anyone who isn't a Christian, you might consider joining a sport or a club or some kind of group where you could develop some friendships with people who don't know Jesus.

Spiritual burnout. We've seen so many Christian school students who view Christianity as just another subject they study at school. They're bored with it. They believe they've heard it all. And this is normal. Throughout history, whenever it's been easy to be a Christian, people often get really bored and lazy with their faith. So if you find yourself in this situation, it's important you actually get out and *live* your faith. Find somewhere in your community where you can put your faith into action by serving other people. Spend time in situations where your faith will be challenged. This will also make you ask good and hard questions that can cause your faith to grow deeper and more alive.

I WAS A MIDDLE SCHOOL DORK! —KURT

Like most eighth graders, I rode my bike to school every day. On this particular day, I was sitting on my bike along the side of the street, just eating a candy bar while I waited for the rest of my buddies to join me. Since just about everyone rode their bikes to school, there was always a big crowd of kids gathered while various groups of friends waited for each other. Did I mention I was in eighth grade?

As I sat there, one of the school bullies rode by me and kicked the front tire of my bike as he passed. Did I mention I was in eighth grade?

As he rode away, I suddenly noticed a bunch of the other kids were snickering and pointing at me. I'd never been in a fight before, but I figured this was a good time to have my first one. Before it was too late, I chucked my candy bar as hard as I could at the bully. Amazingly and—as I was about to find out—unfortunately, the candy bar hit the bully right in the back of his head. He quickly turned around, rode up to me, and pushed me off my bike. It was on!

The "fight" only lasted a few seconds, but it felt like an eternity. Actually, it really wasn't a fight. It was more like a pummeling or a beat-down. Did I mention I was in eighth grade? This guy was tough! He beat the living daylights out of me. It was like I was a piñata, and he was a professional piñata beater—with no blindfold!

I think I mentioned I was in eighth grade, right? The reason this is so important is because the bully wasn't older than me. He wasn't even a fellow eighth-grade student. That's right—I got beat up by a seventh-grade bully!

Fighting is stupid. My parents always taught me that violence is the worst way to solve a problem. They told me nothing good ever came from fighting. They taught me that as an eighth grader, I should be mature enough to walk away when other people wanted to start trouble.

Maybe they should have told me that the worst part about fighting in eighth grade was that you could get beat up by a seventh grader!

SECTION 3
THE PEOPLE YOU
MEET @ SCHOOL

THE CAFETERIA LADY

Out of all the jobs at your school, the cafeteria lady may have the worst one. Think about it—she cooks slop, she serves slop, and then she has to clean up slop. If that's not enough, she also has to put up with a whole bunch of middle school students who seem to have nothing better to do than complain about the slop.

Over the years, the legend of the cafeteria lady has grown. She's been the subject of cartoons, movies, and television shows. If you only judged them by their urban legend status, you'd think every cafeteria lady is a wrinkly, one-toothed, blue-haired, grumpy old lady who gets her kicks from serving mystery meat to innocent young children. (If you're really curious about this, check out chapter 59 next, "Cafeteria Mystery Meat.") Yes, the legend of the cafeteria lady has been around since the beginning of time (or at least since the beginning of cafeterias).

If you eat in the cafeteria, then the cafeteria lady is someone you interact with every single day. Here are a few simple ideas to put a smile on her face:

Say a friendly hello! This sounds like a no-brainer, but we'd be willing to bet she goes quite a while between hellos. Most students are too caught up in their own stuff to remember to say a simple "hello."

Offer a genuine compliment. "This looks delicious" or "Yes! I was hoping we'd have squash today" are examples of little compliments that can make a big difference.

Say thanks. When she plops a big scoop of spinach on your plate, look her in the eye and say a big old "thank you!"

Offer to help. Get permission from your principal to help the cafeteria lady serve food or clean up after lunch. If you offer to help, four things will happen to the cafeteria lady: She'll faint, she'll get back up, she'll gladly accept your offer, and then she'll tell her husband all about it.

This last idea brings up two weird thoughts:

Weird Thought #1: The cafeteria lady is married!

Weird Thought #2: What does the cafeteria lady cook for dinner?

THE SCHOOL BULLY

We wish it didn't happen, but it does. People get pushed around and picked on at school. If it's ever happened to you, you know how scary it can be to spend your school days worrying about having a run-in with a bully. If you've been bullied at school, you aren't alone. One of the growing problems on middle school campuses all across America is bullying.

Bullying usually takes one of two forms. We've got some thoughts on how to handle both types:

EXTREME BULLYING

Extreme bullying needs to be addressed right away. Students who are aggressively violent, running around in gangs, singling out the same victims every day, and so on are examples of what we'd call extreme bullying. So how do you handle it?

First of all, try to avoid the places where these students hang out. If you limit your interaction with extreme bullies, you're less likely to become their next victim. If you know the toughest group of kids on your campus (who punch anybody who walks by) hangs out under the oak tree on the quad—avoid the oak tree on the quad!

Second, if they bother you, don't keep it to yourself. If you become a victim of this type of bullying, be sure to tell somebody like a teacher or a parent about it so they can help you. You might be thinking, Shouldn't I try to be friends with extreme bullies to see if I can help them have a change of heart? Maybe. But be aware it won't be easy and oftentimes the extreme-bully crowd will be tough to get through to.

NOT-SO-EXTREME BULLYING

Okay, that's a dumb name for this category, but it's all we could come up with. This type of bullying is the stuff that's not as violent or dangerous to the victims. It often takes the form of verbal teasing, taunting, and name-calling. Now, even though this type of bullying doesn't hurt physically, it still hurts. While it's super-important to let a grown-up know about extreme bullying, it probably isn't as important with not-so-extreme bullying. You may be able to navigate this type of bully on your own, using some of our expert advice:

First, remember the power of kindness. The Bible tells us not to repay evil with evil (Romans 12:17-18), and it also says that a kind word turns away anger (Proverbs 15:1). In other words, being totally nice to the not-so-extreme bully may be the best strategy.

Second, remember the power of friendship. While extreme bullies often run in groups, the not-so-extreme bully may be someone who doesn't have many friends. She may, in a really weird way, actually be trying to find some people to connect with. We're not saying you have to become best buddies, but we are saying you might want to think about a way you can be friendly toward the not-so-extreme bully.

You won't turn every bully into a poster child for niceness, but you just might be surprised how powerful kindness and friendship can be.

THE JOCK

Every school has 'em: the guys and girls who *live* for sports. You'll find this is even *more* obvious in high school, where sports seem to play a bigger role in friendship groups. Plus, so many middle schools have had to cut school-sponsored sports programs in the last few years that not as many middle school students are viewed as "the athletes" at their schools anymore—not like they were even 10 years ago.

If you're a jock and you believe the sport you play is the coolest thing on the face of the earth, that's great. We encourage you to enjoy your sport and your God-given ability to play. But remember: Other people in your school have things they're *just as* passionate about as you are about your sport. Giving other people the space (and courtesy) of digging whatever they're into doesn't have to take anything away from your enjoyment of your sport.

Just by looking at the pictures of us (Marko and Kurt) in the Introduction to this book, you can see that...well...we weren't jocks. We both played sports, some. But neither of us was really good at them. And NO ONE at our schools would have called us jocks.

If you're like we were—non-jocks—then we have a few tips for you when it comes to those physically gifted, athletic types:

First, remember that jocks are people, too. Yeah, that's a little bit cheesy, isn't it? But, really, it's easy to look at superstar athletes—whether they're professionals on TV or the soccer star in your science class—and think of them as being some-how "better" than you are. Well, they *are* better—at their sport. So what? We all have different gifts. And you're almost-for-sure "better" than they are at some-thing else, whether it's a school subject or a talent or even doing something weird. (Like, Marko can floss his nose—he snorts dental floss up his nose and pulls it out of his mouth—better than anyone else he knows!)

Second, remember that many jocks make sacrifices. It's good for non-jocks to realize that lots of jocks (not all of them) have given up tons of other stuff in order to get really good at their sport. They've often had to sacrifice other things in order to excel in that one thing. That's worthy of our respect, but it can also mean they only think of themselves as someone who plays that sport. It's actually kind of cool—if you have the chance—to help a jock discover other things they can do well.

We live in a culture that's really impressed by people with physical strength and sports ability. That isn't a good thing, really; but it is what it is. Remember, unless the jocks at your school become professional athletes (which almost none can become), they'll start to seem a whole lot more like "normal people" after high school.

THE GOSSIP

Ooh, the gossip. Listen...no, come closer...we have a secret to tell you about the gossip...(just kidding).

Just in case you're not clear what *gossiping* is: It's when you tell stuff—usually rumors, but sometimes real stuff—that the person you're talking about wouldn't want you talking about. The Bible is 100 percent clear about this: Gossip is a sin.

God is clearly against gossip because it hurts people. God loves people and doesn't want them getting hurt. Really, gossip might be fun to share and listen to, but someone's getting hurt in the process.

But this chapter isn't about *you* gossiping. (That is, unless you're "the gossip" at your school—and if you are, stop it!) This chapter is about dealing with the person in every school—actually, there are always lots of 'em—who *loves* to gossip and always has the juiciest bits of gossip to share.

We'll be blunt: This person is dangerous! It's not like you need to worry about them stabbing you in the back with an actual knife. But even if you're friends with the gossip, you'll probably end up getting stabbed in the back with her words. We'd rather deal with a bully than a gossip. At least with the bully, you know when you're going to get hurt.

So avoid listening to the tantalizing morsels of juicy stuff that come spewing from the mouth of the gossip. We know it's not always easy to do this because gossip can be fun to hear. But when you have the chance to listen to gossip, remember the hurt being done to the person who's being talked about. And consider how you'd feel if you were the person being gossiped about.

Also, be careful to avoid giving ammunition to the gossip. You wouldn't "accidentally" give crack to a crack addict, would you? Same thing, man!

Oh, and one more idea that's so crazy-hard to live: If the gossip is gossiping about you, ignore it. Yeah, we know that's hard. But if you ignore the gossip as it spreads, it's more likely to stop and go away (not always, but more often than if you run around trying to stop it).

THE LONER

Every middle school has a loner or two or 10. You see them every day, all over your school. They quietly roam the halls, sit in classes, eat their lunches, and walk home from school. Chances are you've felt like the loner at some point yourself. There's probably no worse feeling than feeling alone and having no one to hang with, talk to, or share life with.

As Christians, Jesus wants us to reach out to the loner, like the way Jesus reached out and befriended Zacchaeus (a very cool story in Luke, chapter 19). Inviting yourself over to the loner's house for dinner (like Jesus did) may not be the best idea, but we do believe there are some other ways you can reach out to the loner at your school:

Say hello. Yep, it can be that simple! Sometimes saying just a simple "hi" and showing you know he exists can mean a ton in the life of someone who's alone.

Ask a simple question or two. Questions like, "What's your name?" "Xbox or PlayStation?" or "What class are you headed to next?" are examples of some easy questions you can ask. There's a chance he might not want to talk to you, but most of the time he does. A simple question can make the loner's day.

Share your lunch. We're not suggesting you give up half your delicious PB & J sandwich or a piece of your orange; give up 15 minutes of your lunch break to sit and eat with somebody who's all alone. This sounds scary, but give it a shot!

Follow up. Don't make it a one-time thing. The next time you come across the loner, follow up with another "hello" or ask a simple question.

Sometimes a person who's alone won't respond the way you think he should. That may be because he actually likes being a loner and finds more joy going through the day on his own. But most of the time, if you reach out to somebody who seems to be a loner, he'll appreciate the effort.

THE GEEK

When I (Kurt) was in middle school, people used a machine called a "word processor." It was the computer of the 1970s because the computer, as we know it today, wasn't around yet. But my family couldn't afford a word processor, so I grew up using something called a "hand." That's right—handwriting was actually cool back in the day.

Even today, I know very little about computers. (I know just about enough to type this paragraph.) What IS a *megabyte*, or a *gigabyte*, or a *take-a-byte*, anyway?

There are tons of middle school students who know all there is to know about computers. They may even know some stuff there isn't to know. They know the latest software and hardware; they know why a PC is better for doing some things, while a Mac is better for doing others. You might call these kinds of people "computer geeks."

So how can a non-geek relate to a geek?

Show an interest in their world. We all love to talk about the things we enjoy doing. I love to surf! When a person asks me about surfing, I can talk to them all day about the ins and outs and the short and long boards of surfing. I guess you can call me a "surf geek." Whether the geek loves computers, video games, or surfing, they usually love to show others what they know. So the next time you need help with your laptop, ask your school's computer geek. He'd probably love to help you, and you might just learn something new!

Realize you have more in common than you think. Like I said earlier, I'm a surf geek. And, if you think about it, we're all geeks at something. What do you love? Do you love *Star Wars* and know everything about Princess Leia? You just might be a *Star Wars* geek. Do you always have to have the latest and best "do-it-all" cell phone? You just might be a cell-phone geek. We may look different on the outside, but on the inside we all have a little geek in us.

Just because others aren't into the same stuff you are, that doesn't make them geeks. Middle schoolers love to label the people they view as being a little less cool as "geeks" or "nerds" because it helps them feel better about themselves. Do you want to feel better about yourself? One way is to recognize that God made you the way he did for a reason, and he did the same thing with all the kids at your school you consider geeky.

THE POPULAR KID

Let's begin this chapter by talking to the few of you readers who *are* the popular kids. Two things:

- Hold it loosely! If you try to hold onto your popularity as if it were your most precious possession, you'll end up hurting people and messing yourself up.

- Spend it! We know that sounds weird, but popularity is like money. You can either selfishly keep it all to yourself, or you can spend it to help other people. In Marko's youth group, a popular middle school girl showed great kindness to a developmentally disabled boy whom everyone else had previously ignored—and it changed everything. Everyone was really nice to that boy from then on. That's what we mean by "spending" your popularity.

Most of us, however, are *not* the popular kids. This chapter isn't about how it's silly to pursue popularity. (Even though it *is* silly.) Nor is this chapter about how it'll eat you alive if you're constantly measuring yourself against popular kids. (But it *will* eat you alive.) And this chapter isn't about how popularity doesn't matter a single bit to God. (But it doesn't.) What this chapter *is* about (finally!) is how to treat the popular kids at school.

So here's our advice:

Don't worship them. Really, it's just crazy how popular people get treated like celebrities. People are always trying to compliment them and cozy up to them in the vain hope that a little bit of their popularity will rub off. C'mon—they're normal people just like you. They need sleep just like you. They get sick just like you. They wake up with bed head and make disgusting smells and have stupid thoughts—just like you (and the rest of us).

Don't be jealous. Jealousy is another one of those things that really seems to tick off God. He does NOT like jealousy—mainly because he knows it will hurt you.

Don't secretly (or not-so-secretly) judge them. We've seen lots of not-so-popular students develop really ugly attitudes about popular kids—hating them even. Don't waste your time with this. Don't decide they're only popular because of this or that. Don't spread rumors about them so you can feel better about yourself.

Just love them like God loves them. God doesn't worship them. And God isn't jealous of them. God just loves them for who they are.

THE RUDE KID

Yup, that kid. The rude kid is *almost* always a guy. This is the kid who burps in your ear when you pass him in the hallway. This is the kid who rips a juicy fart during the math test, and says, "Excuse me!" This is the kid who tells dirty jokes, or pulls your pants down, or pulls his own pants down, or does any one of a hundred other things because he believes it's funny.

Once in a while—let's admit it—the rude kid does something that's actually funny. And often (even if you don't agree), *someone* will think what he did is funny. That's why he does it!

This is really important to understand about the rude kid, and it can totally change your view of him. The rude kid *almost always* does rude things because—deep down—he's insecure and lonely. He wants people to like him and he's learned—because people do laugh when he does some of this stuff—that when he does rude stuff, he gets attention that makes him feel good.

We're not saying you should wait 'til the next time the rude kid does something rude and say, "I feel really sorry for you—you're just doing that because you're a lonely person who needs attention." No, that's not really helpful. But understanding the reality of his life *can* help you show more patience toward him.

If the rude stuff is truly and massively rude, and if it really way-grosses you out (or is stuff that is bad for you to see, hear, or participate in), our advice is avoid, avoid, avoid. This doesn't mean be a jerk to him (because then *you're* being the rude kid). But ignore the rudeness and don't respond to it. If you respond in any way (even just saying, "Oh, you are *so* disgusting!"), then you're actually encouraging him to keep acting that way.

If you get a chance, be nice to the rude kid when no one else is around. You might just find that he could really use a friend and that he's pretty normal—when he's not "performing" for others.

THE PRINCIPAL

Of all the jobs at your school, you probably believe the easiest one is the principal's job. You usually see her hanging out in the distance, watching while everyone else does all the work. She sits in a nice, comfy leather chair in her own private office. She walks around the school every now and then and waves to teachers and students as they walk by (kinda like royalty). And the best part of her job is figuring out creative ways to punish those students who get sent to her office—oh, we forgot, the vice principal gets to do that!

But there's actually more to being a principal than you might think. Believe it or not, even though you might not see it, she works hard and does a lot behind the scenes. She manages the teachers, makes the big decisions, meets with upset parents, and runs the school. She's probably even used a plunger on a toilet or two.

Because of the principal's status, many middle school students think of her as being impersonal. Many are even flat-out afraid of their principals and often think, As long as I stay out of her way, it's all good.

Actually, there are some things you can do to show your principal that you appreciate all she does. Stuff like:

Say "thank you." A simple "thank you" can mean a lot to someone, even a principal. Thank her in person or write her a note saying, "Thanks for being a great principal!"

Give her a birthday card. Write a little card or note wishing her a happy birthday (but first make sure it actually is her birthday).

Stop by her office. You don't have to be afraid of the principal's office. You can actually go there when you're not in trouble. She'd love it if you stopped by to say "hello."

Pray for her. This might sound cheesy, but don't underestimate the power of prayer. Ask God to help your principal make the right decisions for your school. Your principal has a ton of responsibility and prayer can help.

THE SUBSTITUTE TEACHER

There are very few jobs on the face of the earth that are more difficult than being a substitute teacher. We mean very few jobs that someone would actually *choose* to do.

This is helpful to understand: There are usually only two reasons why people choose to become substitute teachers:

1. Because they want to be a teacher but haven't found an open position yet. These people are to be admired and respected because they're choosing a job that doesn't pay as much as other jobs; and they're choosing it, almost always, because they want to help students like you.

2. Because they want the flexibility of a job where they can work some days and not work other days. These people are to be admired and respected because they're choosing a job that doesn't pay as much as other jobs; and they're choosing it, almost always, because they have other things that are really important to them—like a family or other responsibilities.

This is also helpful to remember: A substitute comes into a classroom he doesn't know, sits at a desk full of someone else's stuff, stands before a class of students he's never met before, and teaches a lesson plan he's probably never seen before. And he's either received instructions from the regular teacher, or he's been given nothing and has to come up with something on the spot. Either way, it's seriously hard work.

So here's how you should treat your substitute teachers:

Treat them with respect. They have a killer-hard job! Don't make it worse for them.

Treat them with kindness. Just *one* middle school student treating the substitute nicely can make all the difference in an otherwise very difficult day.

Treat them as you'd like to be treated. Does that sound familiar? We hope so 'cause it's in the Bible! It's called the Golden Rule. (Jesus said it. See Matthew 7:12 or Luke 6:31.)

"I TRY TO BE A 'BLESSING IN DISGUISE' FOR MY TEACHERS, EVEN THOUGH THEY THINK ALL TEENAGERS ARE OUT TO GET THEM."

—RACHEL, 8TH GRADE

THE STRICT TEACHER

One of the things that makes the human race so interesting is that we're all so different. Some people are shy and some are outgoing. Some like to plan ahead and some are spontaneous. Some are structured and some are laid back. Can you imagine how boring life would be if we were all the same?

Believe it or not, teachers are people. (It's true! There was a scientific test done back in the '80s.) And just like the rest of us, teachers come with all different types of personalities. There's the "cool young buddy" teacher, the "old but sweet" teacher, the "wow, this teacher makes learning so *not* like learning" teacher, and of course there's the "totally strict" teacher.

The strict teacher believes fun is a crime. The strict teacher believes smiling is a sign of disrespect. The strict teacher believes excitement is evil. The strict teacher believes rules make the world go 'round. Actually, the strict teacher probably doesn't believe any of that stuff; he just acts like he believes it.

So what *does* the strict teacher believe? Chances are the strict teacher believes the best way to help students learn is to keep control and have firm rules in place. Now, he may or may not be right, but that's not really the issue. The issue is, What do you do about it? Here are a few thoughts:

You have this teacher for only one class period. Out of an entire day of school, you have to sit through his class for about an hour. Don't let one tough class spoil your whole day.

People are different and that's good. Remember, life would be boring if we were all the same—and school would be boring, too. Differences between teachers are part of what makes middle school so fun.

You can't beat 'em, so join 'em! Look, you aren't going to change anything by complaining about how strict your teacher is. The strict teacher isn't going to be overthrown by a mutiny of fun-seeking seventh graders. (Save that for the "cool young buddy" teacher.) The best way to make the most of a class with a strict teacher is to play by the teacher's rules and trust that God will honor your efforts to make the most of what feels like a tough situation.

"I LIKE THE FACT THAT IF I DON'T LIKE MY TEACHER, I ONLY HAVE HIM FOR ONE PERIOD, NOT FOR THE WHOLE DAY."

—JAIME, 7TH GRADE

THE TEACHER'S PET

I (Kurt) can still remember the name of the teacher's pet at the beginning of my sixth-grade year: Andrew. All the teachers loved Andrew. But to the rest of us students, it seemed like Andrew never got in trouble and he always got a break when the rest of us would have been busted for something. Andrew was the first one to volunteer to pass out papers. He was the first one to volunteer to pound the chalk dust out of the erasers. He was the first one to ask a question at just the right time, making it seem like he was really interested in whatever the teacher was going on and on about. Yes, the teachers loved good ol' Andrew, but nobody else did.

While most kids simply disliked Andrew, my feelings for him bordered on hatred. (I don't like to admit that, but it's true.) What did Andrew ever do to me? Nothing. Andrew was a good kid whose only mistake was trying way too hard to get on the teachers' good sides.

One day I couldn't take it anymore. Something had to be done! Now, I'm not much of a tough guy—not now and certainly not when I was in sixth grade. So even though something had to be done about Andrew, I had no idea what that "something" should be. But one day as we were walking between classes, I saw Andrew and I saw my opportunity. I quickly walked up behind him and grabbed his comb out of his back pocket. (Back in those days, guys would actually walk around with big combs sticking out of their back pockets—totally goofy.) As soon as I grabbed the comb, I realized I had no plan for what to do with it next. So I just chucked it onto the roof of the school. Like I said, I'm not much of a tough guy.

The tardy bell was about to ring. So I took off running in one direction, and Andrew took off running in a different direction. It wasn't until about halfway through my next class that I learned in what direction Andrew had run. He'd gone to the principal's office, and now I was about to take a long, slow walk in that direction myself. The principal expressed how disappointed he was in my decision to throw Andrew's comb onto the roof. He ordered me to go to the custodian's office and get a ladder so I could climb up and find the comb. But first I had to call my parents, let them know what had happened, and then ask for permission to climb a ladder.

So what's the point of all this? The point is there will always be kids who work a little harder to win their teachers' affection. Sometimes it'll work and sometimes it won't. Our advice—WHO CARES? Seriously, don't get worked up worrying about how other kids relate to your teachers. Teachers are smarter than they look, and they can usually tell when somebody is being fake or doing dumb stuff to win their attention. You don't need to worry about it because worrying about it may end up causing you to do something dumb yourself.

HOMEWORK AND GRADES

WHY DO MY PARENTS MAKE SUCH A BIG DEAL ABOUT GRADES?

Why? You ask *why*? Because they're *mean*! HA-ha-ha! (evil laughter) No, we're kidding. Your parents are really nice. In fact, they probably bought you this book—so we really like them!

To be truthful, we can't answer this question. So why did you ask it? Oh, that's right. You *didn't* ask it—we wrote it. Stupid us. Anyway, we can't answer it because we don't really know your parents. After all, it's not like they e-mailed us and told us what to write in this book.

But we'll still take a guess because it *is* a question we often hear from middle schoolers. And since we're both dads of middle schoolers now, we're able not only to suppose what *other* parents might be thinking, but we can also tell you what *we* actually believe. So here we go:

We, Marko and Kurt, want our middle school daughters, Liesl and Kayla, to get good grades because we love them. (We love our daughters, that is, not good grades. We only *like* good grades.)

Yeah. Really. That's our reason. It might be hard for you to believe. And other reasons might slide into the picture from time to time—like, sometimes we want our daughters to get good grades because we believe it's a good reflection on us and our parenting; or sometimes we want our daughters to get good grades because we want them to get great jobs and take care of us when we're old. (Older, that is.) But mostly we want our daughters to get good grades because we love our daughters.

We know that if Liesl and Kayla get good grades, it means a few things:

- They're probably actually learning something. And that's a good thing.

- They're learning how to set good priorities and take responsibility for themselves (because we don't do all their homework with them).

- They'll have more options in the future. (See the next chapter.)

WHAT DIFFERENCE DO GRADES MAKE, ANYWAY?

Well, that's a fine question you've asked! (Yeah, we know you didn't really ask it—we did. But humor us—we're older guys.)

We believe the best way to answer that question is to give you (drum roll, please) our tried-and-tested, super-duper, all-perfect two rules about grades. You might also call them "The Deuce":

MARKO AND KURT'S TRIED-AND-TESTED, SUPER-DUPER, ALL-PERFECT
RULE #1

Don't make grades a smaller deal than they are. Sure, you don't have to overreact if you get an average grade. One average grade won't ruin your life. But grades will end up either opening up or closing down options for your future. What we mean is this: If you get great grades, you'll have lots of options in the future (like whether or not to go to college, where you go to college, what career to pursue). And if you get lousy grades, then you *won't* have lots of options in the future. (What college you attend—if you even want to go to college— will be seriously limited, as will your career choices.) So, yeah, your grades matter. Don't pretend they don't, or you're only ripping yourself off.

MARKO AND KURT'S TRIED-AND-TESTED, SUPER-DUPER, ALL-PERFECT RULE #2

Don't make grades a bigger deal than they are. Wait—doesn't that seem to be the direct opposite of what we just said? It's not the opposite—it's more like the other side of the same shiny little coin. Or it's like the other side of the same chicken. Wait—that doesn't make any sense.

Let's get back to grades: If you worry about grades all the time, you can make them an idol (seriously). And God makes it pretty clear in the Big 10 (as in the Ten Commandments) we're not supposed to put anything in our lives in a higher-priority spot than God. If you *live for* grades, you can easily become a messed-up, unbalanced person. It can even make you physically sick.

So there you have it. We don't know what your parents think, but we know what WE think. We think you should keep your grades in their proper place—not too important, and not too *un*-important. Got it? Now get back to that homework!

"BEING BAD IN SCHOOL DOESN'T MAKE YOU COOL."

—TAYLOR, 8TH GRADE

THIS CLASS IS TOUGH!

Almost everyone has a difficult class from time to time. For me (Marko), my toughest class in middle school was the second half of geometry. (That's the kind of math where you look at shapes and angles and stuff like that.) Most kids in my school took geometry for a whole year. Well, in the first semester, I did really well. I've always been pretty good with shapes and stuff, and I was already taking classes in technical drawing (called "drafting"). So my teacher recommended moving me to the advanced placement geometry class for the second semester.

Dude! It killed me! I was suddenly in a class with the smartest kids in the whole school. I went from being a pretty good student—compared to the other kids in the class—to being, like, the *worst* student in the class. I didn't understand any of it. After a few weeks, I begged to be moved back to the "normal kids" class.

It seems there are two main reasons why a class might be super-hard: Either the subject is really difficult (at least for you), or the teacher is really difficult.

If you believe the real issue is a difficult subject, then here are three quick pointers:

- *Don't give up quickly.* Once you've realized the subject is tough for you, it's important to double your efforts, focus, and determination.

- *Talk to the teacher.* This is really important. The teacher needs to know you're trying, but having a tough time.

- *Ask for help.* Ask the teacher, ask your parents, ask another student who seems to "get it."

If you believe the real issue is a difficult teacher, then here are three quick pointers:

- *Quit school and run away.* No, we're kidding—*obviously!*

- *Talk to the teacher—carefully.* It's important to have a conversation (or lots of them) with tough teachers. But we say "carefully" because if you approach the conversation with whining or making a bunch of accusations, you won't get far.

- *Ask if there's a way to rethink the workload.* Maybe there's a way for you to handle the assignments differently. You'll never know until you ask.

- *Find out if you're the only one struggling.* If everyone else in the class is also struggling, then you might need to talk to your parents or seek outside help.

"SCHOOL ISN'T ALL THAT BAD, BUT ALL THE WORK IS A STRUGGLE."

—KELLIE, 7TH GRADE

STUDY TIPS

It usually goes something like this: You're sitting in science class and anxiously waiting for the bell to ring so you can get out of there and on to something more exciting—like pre-algebra. At the last possible moment, your teacher reminds you, "Be sure to study chapters 13 through 15 tonight because we may have a quiz tomorrow." What does she mean by that? Does she mean you should memorize those chapters? Does she want you to reread what you've already read? Does she want you to know every single fact that's listed? Can somebody please be more specific?

Here's a little tip: You'll be surprised by how much information your teachers will share with you if you'll just ask them. Seriously, when you stick around for a minute after class to ask for some help, it shows the teacher you actually give a rip about the class. Teachers have a soft spot for students who like to learn. It's kinda like how Kurt has a soft spot for students in his youth group who bring him doughnuts.

Anyway, chances are your teacher will be happy to explain to you what "study chapters 13 through 15" really means. And it's important to ask because it probably means something different to each teacher. One teacher may want you to review the summary questions at the end of each chapter, while another one may expect you to reread the material and highlight what's important. Still another teacher may simply expect you to be able to remember the big ideas or key facts you learned.

Kurt and I have learned that when our daughters struggle with studying, it's usually because they aren't sure what the teacher expects them to study. So here are two additional super-basic ideas to help make studying a little easier:

Take good notes. Teachers usually quiz and test on the stuff they've lectured on during class. By paying attention and taking good notes, you'll make your study time at home way more effective.

Find a quiet place and give it your full attention. Don't try to study while you're watching television, downloading music on iTunes, talking on the phone, or playing a computer game.

We gotta go now. We need to study for the next chapter we're about to write.

"SCHOOL IS HARD, BUT I JUST TRY NOT TO GET BEHIND, AND I'M FINE."

—BRENT, 7TH GRADE

HOW TO MAKE HOMEWORK NOT SO HORRIBLE

Apparently, going to school for eight hours a day isn't enough. For some reason, your teachers also believe an extra hour or two of schoolwork each night is a good idea. Homework may be the world's greatest invention or the world's worst—who knows? But we do know it probably isn't going away anytime soon.

Before we offer you a few thoughts about making the most of your homework, we thought it might be a good idea to explain *why* you have it in the first place.

A few of the reasons you have homework are—

- 45 minutes of class time usually isn't enough time to understand the concepts.

- Working on your own is a good skill to learn.

- Homework in middle school prepares you for homework in high school, which prepares you for homework in college.

- Your teachers want to ruin your life. Okay, that's not true. Well, maybe it is. No, it's not. But maybe...?

Since homework probably isn't going to disappear, how do you make it not so horrible?

Give yourself less homework to start with. Right now you may be thinking, *Okay, Marko and Kurt, what planet do you live on? I don't give my-*

self homework! Let us explain. Some teachers will give you a few minutes in class to start working on your homework. When that happens, take advantage of it. If you spend those 10 to 15 minutes working on homework instead of goofing with your friends or shooting spit wads at the cute girl, then you will, in fact, be giving yourself less homework.

Do your homework right away. The only thing worse than doing your homework right away is putting it off and worrying about it all evening.

Split it up. If you have a lot of homework, don't try to do it all in one sitting. Work for 20 or so minutes at a time, and then give yourself a break in between to clear your mind.

Reread chapter 2 of this book. You may need to remind yourself that homework is part of the learning process and learning is a really good thing. (Do you remember us saying that back in the second chapter?) If you can see the true value of homework, it might not be so horrible.

GETTING READY FOR A TEST

It's true that some middle schoolers actually like taking tests. But that's just because they like pain. These types of kids also enjoy things like eating liver and onions or going to the dentist. Normal middle schoolers don't like tests. We have middle school daughters, and neither one of us has ever heard one of the girls wake up on a Friday morning and say, "Yes! I finally get to take my English test today! I'm so excited!"

Test taking is one of the most stressful parts about being in middle school. While we won't try to convince you that taking tests will be a ton of fun, we do believe we can give you a few tips to help make the most of your test-taking experiences:

First, reread chapter 28—"Study Tips." Believe it or not, the best way to get rid of test-taking stress is to learn the art of studying.

Next, avoid cramming! When you cram for a test the night before (or the period before!), you add a whole lot of pressure to what's already a stressful situation. The problem with cramming for a test is that, while it may help you pass today's test, it actually hurts you in the long run because you end up forgetting the stuff you crammed for, which hurts the whole learning process thing.

Also, don't cheat. Do everything in your power to resist this temptation. A big problem with cheating is it can become an addictive way of life.

Cheating on a math test easily leads to dishonesty in a whole bunch of other areas.

Finally, after you've put all the other pieces in place, ask God to help. Now, he's probably not going to whisper the answers in your ear, but the Bible does tell us to ask God for help, and he will answer our prayers (Matthew 7:7-8; Philippians 4:6-7; James 5:14-16). If you've studied, if you haven't crammed, and if you refuse to cheat, God will help you remember what you've learned. A prayer before every test doesn't guarantee you'll get an A—God isn't going to do your work for you. But praying before a test *is* a great way to calm your nerves and invite God to be part of the process.

HOW TO DO A LONG-TERM PROJECT

There's an old riddle that goes something like this:

Q: How do you eat an elephant?

A: One bite at a time.

Long-term projects may be the elephants of your middle school experience. They are big, intimidating, hard to get your arms around, and—just like trying to eat an elephant—it's hard to know where to start. So how do you do a long-term school project? One bite at a time.

When you think about it, a long-term project is really just a big homework assignment you hear about way before the due date so you'll have plenty of time to get it done. Because of that, the big tips we can offer you for doing a long-term project are the same as the tips we gave you about how to make homework less horrible. But we do have a few ideas that make extra sense for a long-term project:

If given a choice, choose a topic that interests you. Oftentimes you'll have the choice of what type of book to read for the report, or what country to write about, or what your science project will be. When you're given a choice, choose something you're already interested in and like. Doing a long-term project in an area of interest makes those long, boring hours go by a little more quickly.

Create a time line. Ask one of your parents to help you create a time line that covers the amount of time you've been given and all the various pieces of the project itself. Then create your own list of mini-due dates for all the parts. If you hit each mini-due date, you'll have no trouble hitting the big, final due date for the overall project.

Back up your work! If it's a writing project, such as a report, be sure to back it up by saving it to a separate disc or thumb drive so if something happens to your computer, you won't lose all your work.

Enlist the help of your family. Most teachers allow older brothers and sisters or parents to help out with bits and pieces of big projects. They wouldn't approve of having your dad build your entire science project, but they certainly understand that you're going to need some extra help.

Long-term projects aren't going away, so it's probably best to think of them as an opportunity for learning. Lots and lots and lots and lots and lots of learning! But learning is a whole lot better than trying to eat an elephant.

HOW TO RAISE YOUR GRADE IN THREE EASY STEPS

Ha! Wouldn't it be nice if raising your grades were as simple as doing just "three easy steps"? Really, if we're being totally honest, it's not easy. But here are three things we've noticed that middle school students can do—and you *can* do these three things—that will make a huge difference in your grades:

First, turn in your homework and other assignments on time. Yeah, this seems kind of obvious in some ways. But we're always amazed to know how many students don't do this. Marko's daughter is notorious for getting all her homework done but forgetting to turn it in. And then those homework assignments automatically get marked down to a lower grade whenever they are, eventually, turned in. Middle school is a time when teachers are intentionally trying to get you to take more responsibility for your own stuff. So they often won't remind students to turn in their assignments because they want you to become more responsible. (This is how life in the real world works.)

It can be helpful, if you ever struggle with this, to keep your completed homework and assignments in a specific part of your folder or book bag or backpack—a place where you'll see them when you open it. And seeing them will hopefully remind you to turn them in. If you have completed stuff stashed all over the place, it's a whole lot easier to forget.

Second, make to-do lists. This is a good practice to learn for the rest of your life. Both of us (Marko and Kurt) use to-do lists when we have lots to get done and we can't afford to forget some of it. When you get home from school each day, make a short checklist of the things you have to complete. It's fun to check things off the list, and it gives you a great feeling of accomplishment. But it also helps you remember everything you have to do—even when distractions pop up (dinner, phone calls, that TV show you really want to watch) that can easily cause you to forget something you have to finish.

You might keep an active to-do list in the front of a binder and just add to it throughout the day. That way you don't have to try to remember everything when you get home. Or if your homework is a bunch of projects that aren't due the next day, you could create a to-do list for the week instead. Then if you have math homework every day, for example, just put "Monday math," "Tuesday math," and so on, on your list.

Finally, take notes. Again, this seems really basic. But we're always surprised when we realize how many middle school students haven't learned to do this. When your teacher is talking about a subject, don't just listen. Jot down some notes about the things the teacher seems to think are the most important. The act of writing things down will greatly improve your ability to remember them later on.

> "YOU CAN HAVE A GREAT TIME AT SCHOOL, BUT MAKE SURE YOU HAVE YOUR PRIORITIES STRAIGHT."
>
> —FOSTER, 8TH GRADE

WHEN TO ASK FOR HELP

We often come across middle school students who act like they know everything. They know all about the new clothing styles, their friends, the opposite sex, and even their pet turtles. Lots of 'em even act like they know everything about school. The truth is most people don't know as much as they think they do.

School is a place to learn stuff you don't already know. It's a place where teachers are trained to teach you algebra, the history of the United States, how to write an autobiography, how to solve problems, and even how to paint with watercolors. (There's nothing like a good art class.) So you're busy learning stuff at school all day. And if that's not enough, then your teachers want you to keep learning after you get home by doing that crazy invention called "homework."

Homework can take up a lot of your time, and it can be tough to do, too—especially when you just don't understand it. When it gets tough, what should you do? ASK FOR HELP!

That's right—ask for help. The bummer is many middle school students don't ask. If you have trouble asking for help, there are a few things you should remember:

You're not alone. If you're confused or don't understand something, there's a great chance (like 99 percent) that someone else doesn't understand the instructions, either. You don't understand the instructions for the big science project? You're not alone. So ask for help!

Don't let fear get in the way. We know it can sometimes be super-scary to ask for help. Thoughts might go through your brain like, *People will think I'm stupid* or *I'll be embarrassed because it seems so easy!* or *It's a dumb question to ask* or *I should know this stuff* or *I ask questions all the time.* These are all legit fears that many middle school students have. But it's important to remember that it's okay not to know things. Your teachers want you to learn the stuff they're teaching you, and they're hoping you aren't afraid to ask. So ask for help!

There are people ready to help. There are people in your life who are more than willing to help you out. If you don't want to ask your teacher, there's probably somebody else you can ask who would love to lend a hand. You may be asking, *Who are those people?* We're glad you asked! (See how easy it is to ask?) It can be a parent or relative, an older brother or sister, your super-smart neighbor, or even a kid in your class who seems to understand the stuff you don't.

You're going to be in school for quite a few more years. Being willing to ask for help when you need it is a skill that will help make school a little easier on you.

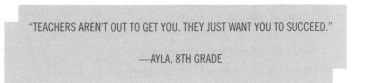

"TEACHERS AREN'T OUT TO GET YOU. THEY JUST WANT YOU TO SUCCEED."

—AYLA, 8TH GRADE

MY MOM WANTS TO GET ME A TUTOR!

Do you know what a *tutor* is? In case you don't, a tutor is just someone who knows more about a subject than you do and who can help you understand that subject better.

We've often heard middle school students complain about getting a tutor. They believe (do you?) that being tutored means they're stupid or they can't figure things out on their own.

Look, if you absolutely *had* to know how to fly a plane next week and all you've ever done is play a computer game where you made Superman fly around a city, it would really be in your best interest to find someone to help you, right? *Not* getting some help would likely end in, well, your final end.

Here's the scoop: Tutors are FANTASTIC! They're nothing to be ashamed of or to feel weird about. Whenever we (Marko and Kurt) need to learn something, we still use tutors in our lives today.

Knowing when to ask for help and then accepting that help when it's offered are major-important character traits to have in life. People who learn to succeed at stuff—anything from learning a school subject to learning how to have a successful marriage to learning how to study the Bible—are people who *love* getting help from others who are more knowledgeable than they are.

If your mom (or dad or teacher) suggests getting a tutor—do it! Run toward it! Consider it a fantastic idea!

If no one suggests getting you a tutor but you're struggling to understand something at school—then ask for help. (See chapter 33 for more on why this is a good idea.) Start by asking your teacher. But if your teacher doesn't have any ideas or doesn't have time (or won't take the time), ask your parent or youth leader for help in finding someone who can help you. Help is good!

I HAVE TROUBLE PAYING ATTENTION IN CLASS

There's nothing worse than going to see a bad movie. You carpool with a group of your friends to the movie theater. You pay your 10 bucks, grab a popcorn and a drink, and 25 bucks later, you're sitting in your seat with great anticipation, watching and waiting for the movie to get exciting. After a few minutes of terrible acting and lousy special effects, you realize it's not going to get any better. So you begin to lose interest. You text message the friend who couldn't make it (and tell him how lucky he is), you whisper to your friends sitting next you, and in extreme cases—you fall asleep.

If you think about it, sitting in a class can be a lot like a bad movie. You pay for books, school supplies, and your school pictures. You walk to class with a group of friends. You grab your seat and feel excited about what the history class has to offer. But a few days in, you realize it's not getting any better, and then you begin to lose interest. You get distracted easily, you talk to the kids around you, and you even fall asleep. But there's one big difference between sitting through a bad movie and sitting through a bad class: You're not going to get a grade for how well you watched a movie.

Since you *are* getting graded on what you learn in class, and since learning stuff in class requires paying attention, then it's a pretty important thing to learn how to do. But how?

Move seats. Sounds really simple, but it works. Ask your teacher to move you away from people who distract you. When you're not super-interested in a class, you're going to be easily distracted. So don't sit next to your friends. Or for you guys, move away from that cute girl you have a crush on.

Move to the front of the class. You're probably thinking, *NO WAY! I can't do that.* Give it try—just a two-week trial. You'll see the whiteboard better, you'll hear everything better, and you'll be much closer to the action (if there is such a thing as an action-packed class). When the teacher is standing only five feet away from you, you're more likely to pay attention. If you don't, she's going to know it. And she'll let you know about it, too.

A little help from your friends. Ask a good friend to keep you accountable. Have him ask you every week about the class that's giving you a tough time. You can also start a little competition with a friend or two who are in the same class. Whoever takes the most accurate, clear, and detailed notes gets anything he wants from the school snack bar—paid for by the losers. To take good notes, you have to pay attention.

Not every class is going to be your favorite. In fact some classes are going to be totally boring. As hard as it may be, it's still important that you pay attention because you'll be tested, and you'll be graded. The more you pay attention in class, the more you'll remember later, the better you'll do on your tests, and the higher your grades will be.

"REALLY, IS THERE ANYTHING WORSE THAN WHEN THE TEACHER CALLS ON YOU, AND YOU HAVE NO CLUE WHAT THE ANSWER IS?"

—MORGAN, 7TH GRADE

I WAS A MIDDLE SCHOOL DORK!
—MARKO

One of my middle school friends was Chris. We seemed determined to do strange, weird things. I'm not sure what it was exactly, but we always encouraged each other to do things that could either get us hurt, in trouble, or both.

Like the time we thought it would be funny to sit on the hood of a guy's car while he gunned the engine. We both flipped up and over the car and landed *behind* it. Chris broke his arm, and I got a concussion. But that's another story.

Or the time we thought it would be funny to jump off the roof of my garage while holding a cheap guitar. And we'd take pictures of the whole thing (including the smashing of the guitar). We damaged some of the shingles on the roof, destroyed the guitar, and were stupid enough to have photos that proved our guilt. But that's another story.

There was one time I spent the night at Chris' house, and we did two really, really stupid things. The first one was at about four in the morning. We thought it would be fun to play soccer in the middle of the normally busy intersection near Chris' house.

There weren't many cars. In fact, we only had to yell, "Car!" and move out of the way about once every five minutes. But there's no question it was completely stupid!

Then, back at Chris' house, it was now about five in the morning and the sun was just starting to lighten the sky. We were bored, and we'd apparently had enough sugar that we still weren't feeling at all sleepy. Chris had some fireworks he'd been holding onto for just such an occasion, so we decided it was the perfect time to light them in his driveway.

What made us think this was a good idea? Uh, because we were dorks!

Of course, the problem was that fireworks are, among other things—LOUD!

About halfway through the second pack of firecrackers (which we'd lit with one long fuse, so the whole pack was going off like a machine gun), the window to Chris' parents' room, which was right above the driveway, flew open. We looked up and saw his mom standing at the window—in her nightgown. She yelled down at us in a voice that absolutely terrified us: "Chris and Marko! What are you *thinking?*! It's five in the morning, and you're waking up the whole neighborhood. Get in the house this *instant!*"

Yeah. As you can probably guess, I didn't get to spend the night at Chris' house for a while after that.

MAKING THE MOST OF
AN AVERAGE DAY

HOW NOT TO BE TARDY

When was the last time you were late for something? Was it last month, last week, yesterday, or today? (Maybe you're running late right now because you're reading this book.) What were you late for? Was it a movie, a youth group meeting at church, your little sister's school play, or soccer practice? Was it your fault that you were late, or was it the fault of the person driving the car?

Some families are never late. Other families are always late. Which family is yours? Not sure? Well, if your mom has a bumper sticker on her car that says, *Better late than never,* then you're probably a member of the "always late" family. We completely understand that sometimes when you're late it's totally out of your control. But getting to class on time is something you can control.

There are several reasons (most of them lame) why a student might be tardy to class. We're going to take a look at how you can avoid most of them:

Wake up! This is tough to do if you're not a morning person. When your mom comes to your room in the morning and says, "Wake up, time to get ready for school," do it! Don't moan and groan, roll over, and then fall back asleep. Be ready to go in the morning so you aren't tardy for your first class. One tip for getting up on time—force yourself to not hit the snooze button.

Wear a watch. Really? You mean on my wrist? Well, without a watch, many middle school students have no way to know what time it is. (Some don't even know what day it is.) Especially when you're out roaming the halls, quads, and athletic fields where there are no clocks. Watches aren't just for nerds anymore, and since you probably don't have a sundial handy, we suggest you wear one. If you don't want to wear it on your wrist, then strap it to your backpack.

Talk later. This is a tough one, but it's probably the biggest cause of tardiness. Most students aren't tardy because they didn't have enough time to get across campus or because they dropped their notebook and spent five minutes picking up their papers. Most students are tardy because they spent four minutes and 57 seconds talking to their friends, and now they believe they can somehow sprint across the campus in three seconds.

The bottom line is that you need to be aware of the time. It's that simple. How long does it take you to get to your next class? How long will it take you to stop by your locker and switch books? How long can you hang out with your friends and still make it to class in plenty of time?

"I LIKE ALMOST EVERYTHING ABOUT MIDDLE SCHOOL EXCEPT THAT STUPID TARDY BELL!"

—JUSTIN, 6TH GRADE

HOW TO MAKE THE BUS RIDE FUN

"The wheels on the bus go 'round and 'round... all day long." Sorry about that. I (Marko) had to get that out of my system. Every time I hear the word *bus*, I can't help but sing that all-time favorite childhood bus song. Be thankful you're just reading the words and not listening to me sing them. (I'm definitely *not* the next *American Idol*.)

Growing up, I took the bus to school, and I didn't really like it. The seats were rock hard and as cold as ice cubes in the morning. There was no heater on the bus, so we just bundled up. If we needed air conditioning, we had to use the standard 53/45 model—53 open bus windows while the bus travels 45 miles an hour. My weak fingers could never seem to press down those levers.

As I think back to my bus-riding days, I've realized that riding the bus doesn't have to be so brutal. Let's take a look at some ways to make riding the school bus a little more fun:

Keep the iPod in your backpack. In other words, talk. Get to know other students on the bus. Say a little "hello" or ask a simple question or two to spark a conversation. I understand that if you're a shy person, talking to someone you don't know is not your idea of fun. But give it a shot. A new best friend might be sitting right in front of you.

Chat with the bus driver. Do you know the bus driver's name? Is he married? What's his favorite sports team? Have you ever said "hello" to him? Just because your bus driver has a comb-over hairdo, that doesn't mean he wouldn't welcome a conversation. Okay, that's an exaggeration. For most bus drivers, the only conversation they have with students is when they ask them to sit down or to quit sticking their rear ends out the window. Maybe you can change that.

Play games. Bring games on the bus you and your friends can play. But make sure they're "travel friendly" first. Picking up 200 Scrabble pieces off the bus floor is not fun. Also keep a deck of cards in your backpack. There's nothing like playing a great game of Go Fish on your way home from school.

Study. Now, I understand this isn't fun. But I wanted to throw in at least one practical idea for how to make the most of your bus ride. You can do last-minute studying for the big test on your way to school. Or you can do some homework on your way home from school so you'll have more time to hang with your friends. Either way, that 30-minute bus ride can be super-productive.

Hey, who said the bus ride has to be boring? The next time you ride the school bus, have fun! And say "hello" to the driver for me.

"AT SCHOOL YOU CAN MAKE IT A GREAT DAY OR NOT, THE CHOICE IS YOURS."

—SPENCER, 8TH GRADE

CARPOOLING WITH BRATS

Before we jump into the carpooling part of this topic, let's come up with a good definition for a *brat*. A *brat* is someone who's annoying, rude, doesn't listen, disrespects authority, and won't shut up. There, how's that? You might have a couple other descriptive words to add to our definition, but that should get you started.

Now, let's talk about carpooling with one or more (OUCH) of these people:

Look at the bright side. It's only for a few minutes out of a very long day. Reminding yourself of this fact can help you survive a tough carpool. Also, you might not realize it, but you're saving your mom time and money. Carpools are set up so parents can share the driving responsibilities. This allows your mom to take your little sister to her school at the same time you're riding in the carpool to your school. So it saves her some valuable time, especially if she has to get to work. It also saves your entire family money. *How?* Well, the less driving around your mom has to do, the less often she'll have to fill up the gas tank. Filling up the gas tank costs money, so carpooling can save your family hundreds of dollars every year. That's pretty cool, and you're doing your part to help pay for that next family vacation.

Listen to music or read a book. There's nothing wrong with not wanting to talk, popping in your earphones, and cranking the tunes. Here's an earphone tip: If someone asks you a question, be respectful and pull out the earphones before you answer. We have an extra health tip for you, too: Don't crank the music too loudly because you could go deaf! If you don't have a portable music thingy, you can always read a book. Try it—it won't kill you.

Love the brats. Brats often feed off other people. If you respond to their tactics in a loud, angry way, they'll only act out more. So the best thing to do is overwhelm them with kindness and gentleness. Talk about what they like to talk about. Listen to the radio station they like to listen to. Smile at them when they purposely spill their sippy cups on your new shirt.

Your carpool probably isn't as bad as you think. (Okay, maybe it is...) Just try to keep a positive attitude, pray, and remember that dealing with brats is a part of this thing called life.

"I USED TO LOOK FORWARD TO THE END OF CAR POOLS. BUT THEN MY MOM STARTED CARPOOLING TO WORK, AND I REALIZED I'LL PROBABLY BE DOING IT FOR THE REST OF MY LIFE."

—BROOKE, 6TH GRADE

FOOD STUFF

We (Marko and Kurt) aren't usually allowed onto many public school campuses, since we don't work there. But when we *have* been allowed on campus, it's usually during lunchtime. Marko used to help out at as a lunchroom volunteer at a couple different middle schools, wiping down tables and stuff like that. So we've seen our share of—the Middle School Lunch Frenzy.

And our experiences tell us that instead of titling this chapter "Food Stuff," it should probably be called "Stuff Food." That's what lunchtime seems to be all about—stuffing in the "food." (We put quotes around the word *food* because some of the stuff you kids stuff in your mouths can barely be considered food.)

At the risk of sounding like parents (uh, we *are* parents, so it's hard not to sound like them), we'll say this: A section titled "Eating Right" could have easily been added to the chapter called "How to Raise Your Grade in Three Easy Steps." Maybe it's not quite that simple, but what you eat has been medically proven—by people a *whole* lot smarter than we are—to have a massive impact on how well your brain works.

Do you ever reach that point in the afternoon, while you're sitting in some random class, when you just can't concentrate? You feel sleepy or distracted. You're not sure if you want to doodle on your paper or take a power-nap. But one thing you're sure of: It's almost impossible to pay attention to what's happening in class.

There are lots of reasons for that—the biggest one being that you're a young teenager, and your body is changing like some kind of mythical warrior beast, morphing from kid to adult. And all that change requires huge quantities of resources from your body, which means there's not much left over for you to use for things like paying attention or concentrating.

But food—glorious food!—can make a big-time difference. And we're not talking about quantity here. Just stuffing French fries or potato chips or chunky cakes-o'-sugar into your belly doesn't help. Those things actually hurt. Greasy and starchy foods (stuff like chips and fries and nachos) make you sleepy, which only makes it harder to concentrate. Sugary foods make your brain bounce around like a rubber bullet in a small room.

We're not nutritionists; but we do know that if you choose to eat veggies and healthy foods, then you *will* *see* a difference in your ability to pay attention and concentrate. It's just a simple fact of how our bodies were designed. And what you choose could cause you to snooze.

> "SOMETIMES SCHOOL CAN BE REALLY FUN, AND OTHER TIMES YOU JUST CAN'T WAIT TO GET HOME BECAUSE THAT TUNA SALAD SANDWICH YOUR MOM PACKED FOR YOU ISN'T EXACTLY AGREEING WITH YOUR STOMACH."
>
> —MORIAH, 8TH GRADE

THE TERROR THAT IS...
THE BATHROOM

Marko here. Man, I can't believe Kurt's making me write the chapter on bathrooms. That was just mean of him! Really, who wants to write about—let alone read about—middle school bathrooms? I mean, most of 'em are straight out of the worst horror movie. And even if they're clean (yeah, right), there's always that awkward weirdness that goes with... well..."using" that room when other people might be in there.

Hey, Kurt and I understand this. I'm still that way. I hate going into public bathrooms. I fly on planes a lot (like, every week), and I almost *never* use the bathroom on a plane—it's like, the *worst*, because it's tiny and weird and everyone sees you going in and coming out.

So...what advice can we give you?

If you're *anything* like us and you want to avoid the terror that is the bathroom, here are a few tips. (I still can't believe we're writing a chapter on this subject!)

First, watch what you eat. In the last chapter, we wrote about how certain foods can make you sleepy or disrupt your concentration. Well, at the risk of stepping into WAY TOO MUCH INFORMA-TION LAND, it's fair to say that those same foods that aren't good for your concentration can also be not-so-helpful here. In other words, if you eat greasy foods, you're *much more likely* to have to...

uh…"go," if you know what we mean. Not only that, but greasy foods lead to the worst kind of "having to go," if you know what we mean. And, really, we *all* want to avoid that!

Second, get in and get out. I mean, sometimes you just *have to* use that place. Find the one on your campus that's less busy than others, or ask your teacher for a pass during class (so you might luck out and find the place empty). Do what you gotta do, wash up, and leave. Keep your head down, and don't make eye contact with anyone. (We're only *kind of* kidding on those last two points.)

Finally, stop to wash your hands. Yeah, we know we sound like your mom or a health teacher right now. But seriously, you just gotta. Really. Don't be nasty. A quick spot of soap, then scrub and rinse, and you can leave feeling clean and germ-free, instead of feeling like you're bringing the bathroom-of-terror with you throughout your day.

And that's all we have to say about that!

THE POP QUIZ—THE SURPRISE THAT'S NEVER FUN

Oh, man, pop quizzes are killer! Last night your parents let you stay up late to watch a movie you'd been dying to see. They were totally cool about this, partially because you'd been good about getting all your homework done all week. But now you're tired, and it's first period, and your mind is numb, and you're just holding out until lunch. Then your teacher says, "Put away your books and get out a pencil; we're going to have a little quiz."

Or, worse yet, you've been so slammed with working on a massive science project about helium that you haven't stayed caught up in *any* of your other classes. (You're also really light-headed because you've been playing with the helium too much.) You know you're seriously behind in history, and you haven't read the book in a week. But you were hoping to get caught up this weekend—after you turn in your science project. But here it is, Friday morning, and your history teacher springs a pop quiz on you. And it's covering all the stuff you haven't read yet.

Let's face it: Surprises in life can either be great or horrible. They're rarely somewhere in the middle. The same thing is true for pop quizzes—and they usually fall closer to the horrible side. We suppose that if you're totally caught up on your work and you've been paying close attention in class and you really understand the topic, then a pop quiz doesn't have to be too bad. But they're *still stressful.*

Here are a few helpful (maybe?) hints:

First, don't panic. Sure, there might be plenty of *reasons* to panic. But panicking doesn't help. In fact, it *always* makes it worse. You can't think straight or remember things when you panic. So try to stay as calm as possible.

Second, take a deep, long breath. Don't freak out and jump right into the quiz. We know it sounds silly, but turn the quiz face down (so you can't see the questions for a moment) and take a minute to breathe, relax, and pray. If you ask God to give you a clear and focused mind, you won't regret it.

Finally, don't be afraid to ask for a retake. If you have some legitimate reason for why you were totally not ready (especially if it's because you had so much work to do for another class and not because you chose to watch TV), then there's nothing wrong with asking the teacher if you can retake the quiz tomorrow. But ask this in private so the teacher has the opportunity to respond only to you. And don't whine. Hey, your teacher might say *no*, but that's the worst that can happen. And you'll never hear a *yes* if you don't ask.

I SIT NEXT TO SOMEBODY I DON'T LIKE

We hear this one from middle school students all the time. Usually when we hear this, the student is complaining that the person sitting by them makes the class more difficult. We know there are lots and lots of reasons why this might be true. But we believe they all break down into one of two main issues:

Reason #1: I don't like sitting next to this person because he's a jerk.

Maybe the person sitting near you is a bully who picks on you all the time. (Make sure you read chapter 14 on how to deal with bullies.) Or maybe the person sitting near you is gross and says and does disgusting things all the time. (Make sure you read chapter 20 on how to deal with a rude kid.) Or maybe the person sitting near you tries to copy your work all the time or tries to talk to you, which gets you in trouble.

No matter what the issue, we believe you have only two choices: love and stay, or love and leave. Huh? We'll explain. Either way, no matter how much a person bugs us, we're commanded to see him as one of God's creations and as someone God loves. That's not always easy to do, we admit. But try to think of the person as Jesus would. Then you can either stay where you are and focus on how to respond to that person with love, or you can ask the teacher to move you to a different seat. (If you choose the second option, don't do it in a mean way.)

Reason #2: I don't like sitting next to this person because I'm a jerk.

We're always a bit surprised by how often this turns out to be the real issue, even though students never believe it is. The truth is they don't want to sit by someone because that person will hurt their popularity, or because that person is a "loser," or because that person "smells funny," or whatever. Get over yourself. If this is you, then maybe *you're* the somebody that other people don't want to sit next to. (See Reason #1.)

SECTION 6
THE P.E.PUZZLE

I HATE THE P.E. UNIFORMS *(AND SCHOOL UNIFORMS)*

Really, it's not only the clothes some of you have to wear for gym class, right? Lots of schools all across the country and around the world are finding that school uniforms are really helpful for decreasing violence and decreasing problems with students wearing clothes that are a distraction or otherwise inappropriate.

So you might be bugged by the shorts and T-shirt you have to wear for gym class. Or even more, you might be bugged by the uniform you have to wear to school.

Here's the upside to remember: Everyone else is wearing it also.

No, seriously. It might be awkward to wear those gym clothes or school uniforms if you were the *only* one who had to wear them. But when *everyone* has to wear them, it's not really that big a deal, right? At least it's not as big a deal as it would be if *only you* had to wear them. Man, that would really stink!

While you might think it's a total pain in the behind to wear clothes you would *never* choose for yourself, there are some great advantages to everyone wearing the same thing:

First, it means you don't have to worry about what you wear. I (Marko) remember a student who was a super-popular middle school guy. I once asked him what caused him stress. He thought about it for a minute, and then he answered (to my surprise), "What to wear to school. Every morning and every night I stand in front of my closet and wonder if what I wear to school will cause people to like me less." Now, that's pretty sad; and we hope you aren't that extreme. But when everyone gets to wear whatever they want, there *is* a lot of pressure to look a certain way or to have the right brands or to have new stuff (or old stuff, or whatever's in style). School gym clothes (and school uniforms) do away with that kind of pressure.

Second, gym clothes and school uniforms are the great equalizer. That just means everyone is equal when it comes to clothes. And that can make it easier for you to make new friends. Think about it, in schools where they *don't* wear the same gym clothes (or have school uniforms), kids in certain groups of friends all dress the same way. That's just one more (likely expensive) hurdle you'd have to get past if you tried to make a new friend.

One more thought—without P.E. uniforms, you'd probably get all sweaty and smelly from running laps in your school clothes, right? Who wants that?

I HATE CHANGING IN FRONT OF PEOPLE

We (Kurt and Marko) never go inside school locker rooms, but we do go on enough overnight trips with middle school students (like, to camps and retreats and mission trips) to know how awkward it is for most middle school students to change in front of each other.

We've seen our share of guys (since, you know, *we're* guys) change their clothes while they're still *inside* their sleeping bags at camp. We sure don't have the skill or flexibility to do that. But then, we're old and our bodies don't move that well.

Here's the main thing to understand about this: *Almost all* middle school students feel this way. In other words, you're normal if you feel awkward about changing in front of other people. There are always a few kids who will change in front of anyone and prance around in their underwear like they *want* you to notice them. These are usually the guys who've already grown into more adult-like bodies or the girls (or guys) who are young enough not to be aware of the potential awkwardness. But most kids find it awkward.

That's because your body is changing so much right now. Really, your body changes more during your young teenage years than any other time in your life—other than the years between your birth and your third birthday. And all those physical changes usually make a person wonder if her body is normal. We've heard this from thousands of male and female middle schoolers. Most feel like their bodies are somehow not quite normal; they think they're too skinny or too chubby, too tall or too short, too something or too whatever. Just know this: All the other kids who are changing around you feel the same way.

So what can you do? Our advice is: Prepare and execute. What we mean is this: If you want to get changed quickly (the "execute" part), then you have to be prepared. Make sure you have all the clothes you need to change into. There's nothing worse than being stripped down to the outfit you were born in, only to realize you don't know where your undies are. So get it all ready first, then quickly—but not so quickly that you look like a speed-freak and draw more attention to yourself—make the change.

Yeah, this can be awkward. Just remind yourself: *Hey, even when I'm down to my undies, it's not much different than going to the beach.*

"THE BEST PART OF MIDDLE SCHOOL: P.E. THE WORST PART OF MIDDLE SCHOOL: CHANGING FOR P.E."

—SANDRA, 6TH GRADE

I ALWAYS GET PICKED LAST

P.E.—you either love it or hate it. If you're an athlete and like physical activity, then you probably love it. If you're not an athlete and therefore don't like doing anything involving physical activity or some kind of ball, birdie, or puck, then you probably hate it.

Unfortunately, a big part of P.E. is the process of picking teams. The only people who typically *like* picking teams are the people who always get picked first; everybody else hates it. And nobody hates it more than the guys and girls who seem to always get picked last. It's no fun being last, whether it's your winless soccer team or getting picked last for the P.E. dodgeball tournament. It can be super-embarrassing and can really affect the way you feel about yourself. If you find yourself getting picked last for P.E. teams, here are a few things to remember:

Remember that P.E. class is not everybody's favorite. Not everyone likes sports, and that's okay. Not everyone likes competition, and that's okay, too. Not everyone likes running around and working up a sweat, and that is totally fine. People dislike P.E. for a variety of reasons—*I'm not an athlete, I'm not a fast runner, The mile stinks, My P.E. teacher is a wacko.* You don't have to like P.E., but giving a little extra effort may be all it takes to get a little better at some of that "P.E. stuff." And getting a little better might be all it takes to keep you from getting picked last every time.

Ask the teacher if there's another way to pick teams. Like we said, it's not fun to get picked last. The best way to avoid getting picked last is to come up with another way to assign teams. There are lots of other ways to create teams without having team captains pick them in front of the entire class. Ask the teacher if any of these alternatives can be used:

- The teacher puts the teams together before class starts.

- The teams are randomly created by giving each student a number or drawing names from a hat.

- The teacher picks three students at a time to form teams so no individual student is last picked.

Nobody likes to get picked last. But it's important to remember that in life's big picture it doesn't really matter how quickly you get chosen for a team. God made you, and he loves you no matter when you get picked.

WHY DO THEY MAKE ME RUN THE MILE?

There are some sick, twisted people in this world, and they do strange things that don't make any sense. One of these strange things is running. Neither of us can figure out why people would run on purpose—for fun. When you get into high school, some students will join the cross-country team. We know, it doesn't make sense to us, either, but it's true.

Do you know what *cross-country* means? Well, let's break it down. In ancient Greek the word *cro* means "to run" and *sscountry* means "without purpose." So *cross-country* means "to run without purpose." Okay, maybe that's not really true, but it sure seems true.

The mile is a form of cross-country race. Actually, the mile is a race that many people run professionally, and you can watch it every four years during the summer Olympics (except nowadays it's the 1,500 meters). But if you have no desire to run the mile when you grow up, why do they make you run it in P.E. class? Here are a few answers to this puzzling question:

It's some sort of law. It's probably not an actual law, but having students run the mile is one of the standard P.E. things that schools are expected to follow. Your state and our federal government have all sorts of expectations about what gets taught at school. Believe it or not, they actually have guidelines about running and stuff that your school needs to pay attention to.

It's called "P.E." for a reason. Not sure if you know this, but "P.E." doesn't really stand for "please exclude" me from running the mile. It stands for "physical education." So your P.E. teacher is there to educate you about all kinds of stuff that's physical. Unfortunately, running the mile is part of that stuff. You don't run (or walk) the mile just to do it, but you do it to learn how your body responds to different types of physical activity.

It's good for you. We know you didn't want to hear this one, but it's true! Running, whether it's one mile or a marathon, is good for you. Your body needs physical activity, even at your young age. Exercise isn't something that only your parents need as they get older and wider.

The mile isn't going anywhere. It's been around ever since people started measuring stuff. Making middle schoolers run a mile at a time has been around for a long time, too. We both did it; and if you have kids someday, they'll be doing it, too.

STUFF YOU MAY NOT HAVE LEARNED IN MIDDLE SCHOOL: ELEPHANTS ARE THE ONLY ANIMALS THAT CAN'T JUMP.

DODGEBALL STRATEGIES

Oh my, what a great game! It's been played for years and years throughout elementary and middle schools across the nation. But in recent years, it's become more popular than ever. People all over the world are playing dodgeball in record numbers. Dodgeball isn't just a playground game anymore. Believe it or not, there are actual dodgeball leagues for teenagers and adults to join.

So how do you become a dodgeball dominator?

Be aggressive but cautious. You want your opponent to fear you! You do this by attacking, and you attack by throwing the ball as hard as you can (at an opposing player of course). But as you aggressively attack, you must always keep an eye (or two) out for the ball being thrown at you by your opponent. The key word here is "watch." You must keep your eyes open and never turn your back or head away from your opponent. NEVER!

The ball is your friend. Use the ball for more than just throwing. A key part of the game, which many players forget, is to catch the ball your opponent throws at you. Sometimes all you can do is dodge, but more times than you might think, you can catch the ball instead. This strategy is even more important if you have no dodging skills. (A real bummer since the game is called *dodgeball*.) You can also use the ball to block. When you're holding a dodgeball, hold it with both hands and use it to deflect or knock away any ball that comes your way. But make sure you keep a tight grip on it. If you drop your ball, you're out.

Communicate with your teammates. Communicating in dodgeball is a very important team strategy. This requires talking—and loudly enough for your teammates to hear. This could be saying stuff like, "Watch your left!" or "Cover me!" or "That was awesome when you pegged that guy in the face!"

Play with style. Whether you dominate or stink up the court, it's important to always look good. *How do I look good?* you ask? Invest in a good headband and a wristband or two. And wear a good pair of long tube socks that don't match anything else in your dodgeball ensemble.

The most important thing to remember as you play this great game is not to argue with your teacher or whoever is serving as the referee. When you get hit, quietly walk off the court. When you hit someone else, don't point at her and rub it in her face. Bad sportsmanship isn't fun, and everyone deserves to have a good time.

I WAS A MIDDLE SCHOOL DORK!
—KURT

It was a hot summer afternoon, and I was just sitting around my house—bored. So I decided to ride my bike over to my friend Mike's (so I could sit around *his* house—bored). I lived several miles away from Mike, so riding to his house on a hot day really wore me out.

By the time I arrived, our friend Eric had decided to join us. Eric and Mike were hanging out in the living room, talking sports. We loved sports. We ate, drank, and slept sports. And on a day like that one, since it was too hot to be outside playing sports, we could spend hours just talking about sports. As usual, the conversation bounced from sport to sport, player to player, and topic to topic.

Things were going fine until the topic switched to baseball. The specific topic: Who is the best baseball team? We were all Anaheim Angels fans, but the Angels were terrible that year. (Now they're the "Los Angeles Angels of Anaheim" and actually won the World Series in 2002.) Anyway, it's important to understand that I was a different type of fan than Mike and Eric. I was the kind of fan who believed my favorite team was *always* the best team. It didn't matter if they were terrible; they were my favorite team, and therefore, they were the best. Mike and Eric, on the other hand, were the kind of sports fans who believed the best team was whichever team happened to play the best that year. If their favorite team stank, they'd admit it and award the "best team" title to a team who actually deserved it.

Needless to say, the discussion quickly became an argument because I refused to admit the Angels weren't the best team in baseball. Mike and Eric insisted the best team that year was the Oakland A's. The A's had a much better team, much better players, and a winning record to back up their claim. But I still refused to admit the A's were better than the Angels, so the discussion-turned-argument was now an all-out fight!

My rage suddenly got the best of me, and I stormed out of Mike's house. I was so angry, I started walking home, and I didn't stop until I got to my front porch. But as I was unlocking the door, I suddenly remembered I'd left my bike in Mike's front yard. I'd been so mad that I'd completely forgotten about my bike and walked several miles in the scorching sun—all the way home. So I turned right around and walked several miles in the scorching sun *back* to Mike's house.

When I got there, Mike and Eric were now hanging out in the front yard. Without even looking at them, I hopped on my bike and rode away shouting, "Angels rule!" at the top of my lungs.

THE UGLY SIDE
OF MIDDLE SCHOOL

CHEATING

Gee, what do you think we're going to say here? Think we'll say, "Hey, cheating isn't that big of a deal. Everyone needs a little extra help from time to time!"

Uh, yeah. Or, no.

Of course you know we're going to tell you cheating is a lousy idea, and it's not what students who are followers of Jesus should be about. But you already know that. So we won't spend the whole chapter telling you again.

We *will* write this: You know and we know (surprise!) that cheating in middle school (and even more so in high school) is so common that most students do it (at least once in a while) without thinking much about it. Most students believe it's just the way the game is played. What makes it so tough for students who are committed to doing the right thing (*not* cheating) is that students who get away with cheating end up getting good grades when you (who choose *not* to cheat) don't get as good a grade.

Did you know people have struggled with this unfairness forever, and the Bible even talks about it? Check out the prophet Jeremiah's complaint to God:

YOU ARE ALWAYS RIGHTEOUS, O LORD,
WHEN I BRING A CASE BEFORE YOU.
YET I WOULD SPEAK WITH YOU ABOUT YOUR JUSTICE:
WHY DOES THE WAY OF THE WICKED PROSPER?
WHY DO ALL THE FAITHLESS LIVE AT EASE? (JEREMIAH 12:1)

When God responds to Jerry, he basically says, "Jerry. Dude. Don't you know that I see this? And don't you know that I'm going to sort it all out?"

See, here's the deal: It may feel like people who cheat still get to win. After all, they get good grades, they don't have to study, and they don't get caught (usually). There don't seem to be any consequences to their actions, either. But God is asking you to trust that he sees your good deeds (*not* cheating) and there *will* be consequences on both sides—good consequences for you (for *not* cheating), and bad consequences for cheaters.

FIGHTS

If you're a home school student, then you probably don't have to worry about fights too often. (We're talking about physical fighting here.) That is, unless you have a sibling who's also homeschooled or a really mean pet.

But most students in most schools see fights break out once in a while. I (Marko) still remember the day in sixth grade when a girl kicked my rear end and made me cry. It was not a good day. (She was a *really* big girl, by the way, so shut up!)

We believe there are three kinds of middle schoolers when it comes to fighting. There are those who kinda like to fight; those who will avoid a fight no matter what; and those who don't want to fight, but might end up fighting someone at some point.

To those who kinda like to fight, we say: Pick a sport, man! You clearly need to get out some aggression. Doing something really physical, like running around a basketball court or whaling away in a karate class, can take care of that need. Then you can avoid sin, get your aggressive chuckles, and stay out of trouble. Seriously.

To those who will avoid a fight no matter what, we say: Good for you! Don't feel like a wimp. Strength is measured in lots of ways, not just by whether or not you can pound on someone. Real strength often shows up in knowing how and when to *avoid* a situation that will ultimately cause problems for everyone, solves nothing, and is the opposite of what God wants for us.

And to those who don't want to fight, but might end up fighting someone at some point, we say: It's never too late to call it off. We were both in this camp. You might find yourself super-angry, or getting hit, or getting drawn into a fight by something else. Just remember this bit o' wisdom: You *always* have a choice. The other person might tease you for walking away from the fight, but so what? You'll show a whole different kind of strength by walking away.

PEER PRESSURE

Ask 100 middle schoolers what one of their biggest struggles is and almost every one of them will mention peer pressure. Peer pressure is part of just about everybody's life, but it seems to hit its peak in middle school. Why is peer pressure so tough to handle? Well, just think about it for a minute: It's pressure put on you by your peers. There are few things tougher in life than trying to go in one direction when it seems like everybody else is going the opposite way.

Daniel was a young dude in the Bible who faced a TON of peer pressure. He and a whole bunch of other young people were kidnapped from their homeland and forced to live in a foreign country far, far away under the rule of a ruthless king. One day, the king decided to pass a law making it illegal to pray to anybody but him. It was like he declared himself God. While everybody else decided it would be best to obey the new law, even though many of them knew it was wrong, Daniel refused to give in to the pressure. He refused to pray to the king and kept on praying to God.

When the king became aware of Daniel's courage and his refusal to give in, he decided to do something about it. Guess what he did? He tossed Daniel into a den full of hungry lions. Now, you'd probably guess that this story has a bloody, gruesome ending. But you'd be wrong. God was with Daniel. He protected Daniel by closing the mouths of the lions and keeping Daniel from becoming a tasty meal. When the king saw this, he had Daniel pulled out of the pit. And then the king admitted he'd made a big mistake. (You should read the whole story in the sixth chapter of the book of Daniel sometime.)

There's nothing easy about dealing with all the peer pressure you feel at school. In fact, sometimes you might feel like you'd rather be tossed into a den full of hungry lions. Saying "no" to peer pressure is tough, risky stuff. Think how much easier it would have been for Daniel to just go with the flow and do what everybody else was doing. But he knew who he was and what he believed in. Daniel stood strong in the face of crazy peer pressure; and by doing so, he allowed God to show up in an amazing way. God wants to do the same thing for you.

MEAN KIDS

There are mean kids everywhere. It doesn't matter where you live or what kind of school you attend, there's bound to be a mean kid or two lurking somewhere, just waiting to make your life miserable. Sooner or later, we all have to deal with a mean kid.

Here's the thing to remember whenever you're confronted by a mean kid: *Almost every* mean kid is mean for a reason. In other words, there's usually some part of her life story—that you may or may not know—that offers some explanation for why she's a mean kid.

That's not to excuse her meanness or to say it's no big deal. It IS a big deal when someone says or does something mean to you. And we're not trying to say it's easier to deal with if you just remember that mean kids are mean for a reason.

But, for example, if you knew the mean kid was mean because his dad beats him all the time, or because his mom is an alcoholic and he can't do anything about it, or because he feels stupid, well, that might cause you to think differently about him, wouldn't it? If you knew the mean girl has a mean dad who's always told her she's good for nothing, or that she was raped by an uncle three years ago, or that she has an older sister who constantly tells her she's ugly, well, wouldn't that give you a little more understanding toward her?

We're not suggesting that every time a middle school student does something mean it's because she's had major trauma in her life. But a kid who is regularly mean—like, all the time—is usually that way for a reason.

We're not asking you to ignore the meanness or to let someone treat you like dirt. What we *are* asking you to do is to consider the possibility of something going on *behind* the meanness. Hopefully that insight will give you the same perspective Jesus has when he looks at the mean kid. Jesus isn't happy about the mean stuff; but he's even more saddened by whatever it was that made the kid mean in the first place.

Maybe you can try to be understanding and patient also.

DRUGS

When you consider the possibility of drugs being available in your middle school, you might think, *Yeah, of course.* Or you might think, *What? No way! Not at my school!*

We really hope you won't have to worry about drugs in your school; or at least that they won't be an issue among the circle of students you hang around with. But we'd be crazy if we didn't mention them.

A pair of stories...

I (Marko) once heard a youth speaker give his testimony to a group of middle school students— and I've heard this kind of thing lots of times. He talked about how he did every kind of drug imaginable when he was in middle school and high school, and how God saved him from all that. Now, that's all nice and good, really; but he shared way too much information. Afterward, I was talking to a nice, clean-cut, sweet little seventh-grade girl. She said to me, "I mean, if he could do *all of that* and now he's, like, a Christian speaker and all... it seems like it might be okay for me to just try a couple things, and I'd be okay, too. I mean, I just want to know what it's like."

Recently, one of the guys in my seventh-grade small group shared from his heart how sad he was about one of his friends who got busted for pot (marijuana). Even though the guy in my group didn't *do* drugs, he was still impacted by them.

The Bible makes it clear that evil will always be with us—until Jesus returns. And there's no question that drugs are a part of that evil.

You probably know this already, but we're going to say it anyhow:

- Can you try drugs and still honor God with your life? *No.*

- Can you try drugs—any kind (pot, speed, ecstasy, anything)—once or twice and not get hooked? *Maybe. But maybe not.*

- Can you try drugs and not mess up your life? Or not get into trouble? *Maybe. But maybe not.*

- Is there ever a good reason to try drugs—ever? For ANY reason? *No, absolutely not.*

And what should you do if you become aware of someone you know using drugs? Well, if you care about how *they'd* answer any of the questions above, then you'd say something, tell someone, do something. Yes, it *is* your business. Yes, it *is* your problem.

DRINKING

Have you heard this one? An ostrich walks into a bar...

No, sorry, we're not going to tell a joke. Too bad, huh? It would be nice if we knew a good one!

We thought about combining the chapter on drugs with the chapter on drinking because, in many ways, what we have to say to you about the two topics is very similar:

- We know both drug use and drinking are common in middle school.

- We expect you'll have to deal with one or both of them at some point, if you haven't already.

- Neither one is what God wants for you, and they totally aren't worth the risk of addiction or other problems.

But even so, there's still enough to say about drinking (you know we're talking about drinking alcohol, right?) that we thought we should keep the chapters separate.

Drug use in middle school isn't quite as common as drinking is—not yet, anyway. The average age for boys to try their first taste of alcohol is 11 years old; the average age for girls is 13 years old. That means before they turn 12 years old, half of all boys will have tried alcohol; and by age 14, half of all girls will have done so. You're about that age, aren't you?

We're not suggesting that if you haven't tried alcohol yet, then you'd better get around to doing it quickly. Just the opposite—the longer you wait, the more likely it is that you WON'T have a problem with alcohol at any time in your life. So if you're in the "haven't tried it yet" category, that's a really good thing.

People—even Christians—differ in their views of alcohol. You might live in a home where there's no alcohol—ever. You might live in a home where alcohol is present in a moderate amount. Or you might live in a home where alcohol is abused. (If this is the case, you have to be *extra-super-cautious* because you're a prime candidate to abuse alcohol also.) But one thing is very, very clear: Alcohol use by teenagers is *never* good, *always* harmful and risky, *always* against the law, and *always* to be avoided.

If you choose not to drink at all, you might get teased or pressured (depending on the kids you hang out with). But that doesn't mean it's not a good choice. People who make bad choices often tease people who make good choices—it helps them feel better about their bad choices.

GANGS

For some of you, gangs are something you see only on TV or in movies. But for others, gangs are a present reality in their everyday lives.

We're not talking about groups of friends, as in, "This is the gang of friends I hang out with." We're talking about violent groups who exist to protect each other and hurt others. Sometimes these groups are formalized, have names, and may even have connections with groups in other schools and neighborhoods. And sometimes they're less official—just a violent group of kids who mess with people.

We're guessing that very few of our readers are being tempted to join a gang. But if that *is* you, then please, please talk to your youth leader or another adult who cares about you.

But for most of you, the only attention you'd typically pay to gang members is trying to avoid them.

A couple things to remember:

- We live in a really violent world. And we live in a culture that loves violence (just think about all the violence on TV, in movies, and in video games). All this violence in our world, as well as our "love" of violence, is *part* of the reason why gangs exist.

- Try to think of kids in a gang as Jesus would think of them: as teenagers he loves and cares about. Jesus talks about the shepherd leaving the 99 sheep to find the one lost sheep (Matthew 18:10-14). That's how Jesus feels about a gang member. In other words, fearing them is normal, but hating them is not an option for middle schoolers who are followers of Jesus.

A couple things you *can* do:

- Pray for gang members. There are thousands of stories of ex-gang members who've had their lives turned upside down by Jesus. If you know of gang members in your school, pray for 'em.

- Be friendly. It's amazing how tiny bits of niceness can be such a surprise to people. Find ways to be kind. However, this is best lived out with individuals, not with an entire group of gang members.

FEELING LEFT OUT

Just sitting down to write this chapter made us feel a little sad. It makes us sad because we know how much it hurts to feel left out. And if you're feeling that way, we want you to know we understand how you feel because we've both felt that way before. We've also talked to lots and lots of middle schoolers who feel that way, too. Feeling left out is no fun.

We may not know the exact reason why you're feeling left out, but we do know a few of the common reasons why it happens:

Middle schoolers are selfish. Most kids your age are way more worried about their own survival, popularity, friendships, and so on than they are about yours. Because being in middle school is so tough, it's pretty common for middle schoolers to overlook the needs of their classmates because they're just too busy looking out for their own needs. In other words, sometimes people leave out other people not because they're trying to be mean or hurtful, but just because they aren't thinking about the other person at all.

Middle schoolers move in herds. What we mean is that most kids your age like to hang out with and spend time with other kids who look, act, and dress like them, and who do the things they like to do. It's super-easy for them to leave out other kids if they don't believe they have a lot in common with them.

There are lots of other reasons, but those two are probably the biggest. So what do you do when you feel left out? Well, to be honest there's no easy answer to that, but here are a few thoughts:

Be yourself. Don't try to be somebody you aren't, just to fit in. Trying to change who you are will usually backfire on you. The people you're trying to fit in with can tell you're trying too hard, and they may end up leaving you out even more.

Be friendly. There's a verse in the Bible that says one "who has friends must...be friendly" (Proverbs 18:24, NKJV). Sometimes people who've been left out a whole lot start to respond by shutting others out, treating them poorly, and acting like they really don't care. This just results in a crazy cycle of being left out even more.

Be an "includer of others." If you're feeling left out, you aren't the only one. What if you decided to find other kids who also seem to be left out and include them? Pretty soon you'd have a group of friends who no longer feel left out because now you've all been included—by each other. Pretty cool stuff!

Know that you're never alone. We know this sounds a lot like two middle school pastors talking, but remember that even if you feel alone, you aren't. God is with you; he's on your side and he wants to help you figure out this whole middle school thing.

BEING THE NEW KID

No one wants to live life alone. (Look back at chapter 17—"The Loner.") God has wired us to share life with other people. When you're the new kid at school, especially when you move in the middle of the school year, you don't know anyone, you don't know where anything is, and you can totally feel alone. As the new kid, you need to know that you can't just sit at your desk or at the lunch table and expect others to come to you and ask to be your new best friend. You gotta be proactive, take that first step, and look for opportunities to get to know others. So what are some things you can do as the new kid on campus?

Be nice. As you wander around your crowded middle school campus, make sure you're nice. It seems like a no-brainer, but over the years we've seen many middle school students try to fit in by being rude, sarcastic, and outright mean. Don't build a friendship on this stuff. Just be nice, smile, be encouraging, and ask a lot of questions. Being friendly is the best way to make friends.

Look for a few people to eat lunch with. As the new kid, one of the best times to get to know others at your school is during lunch. Lunch is 30-plus minutes of uninterrupted quality time for you to connect with others at your school. Walk around campus and look for someone you've met in class, on the bus, or out in the halls, and then ask if you can eat lunch with her and her friends. Chances are good (probably like 86.2 percent) that she'll say "yes." But if she says "no," don't take it personally.

(She doesn't even know you.) Stay positive and find another group to hang out with. When you do find a group, make sure you're nice.

Be patient. When you're new to a school, it's super-tempting to get frustrated if you don't make friends right away. Be patient. It's probably going to take a little while for everybody else to get to know you and for you to "click" with a group of friends. Remember, most of the kids at your new campus have known each other forever, so adding somebody new to their group takes a little time.

Even though we tried to make being the new kid sound easy by listing three simple steps, we know it's a big deal. If it's ever happened to you, you know what we're talking about. But hang in there...you're only new for a little while.

SCIENCE CLASS

You might think it's weird that we're including a chapter on science class in the section called "The Ugly Side of Middle School." No, it's not because we hate science. (Although Marko did have a horrible experience in tenth-grade chemistry. The teacher was so bad that when a 200-point test was given, the average score in the class was 12. Really.) The reason why science is included in our "ugly side" section is because it's the one class where Christian teenagers often struggle a bit.

If you go to a Christian school, then this is unlikely to be an issue for you. But for public school kids, there's often a tension during science class because so much of science is built on the assumption that there is no God. And we realize this can happen in any subject, like if you have an English teacher who believes Christianity is stupid and decides to make a big deal out of it. (We both had teachers who did this.)

In any case, science class doesn't *have* to be this way—there are lots of great scientists who are Christians. And those of us who *do* believe in God and follow Jesus also believe God invented the whole world and all the stuff that science is trying to explain anyhow—so it's all good.

The most common area of science class where Christian students find a challenge is in the discussion of evolution. Evolution, in case you haven't studied it yet, is an explanation for how the world came to exist. There are Christians who believe in the evolutionary process *and* believe God invented the world. But most science books (and science teachers) present the beginning of the world as something completely random—a wild and lucky bit of chance. And *some* science teachers (not all of them) really like to push Christian students by "proving" how stupid the students' beliefs are. Of course, those science teachers know a lot more than most middle schoolers do, so this can be tough.

Our quick advice:

1. Don't be embarrassed by what you believe.

2. Don't be intimidated by a teacher who wants you to believe the idea of God creating the world is stupid.

3. Don't be a jerk when you face stuff like this. It doesn't help at all, and it isn't honoring to God to be mean or angry in response—just stay cool.

4. If you find yourself having real doubts and questions—that's okay. In fact, it's good. Just make sure you talk to someone you trust, like a youth leader or pastor or your parents. We all need to talk about these things and get help sorting them out.

SECTION 8
MIDDLE SCHOOL
URBAN LEGENDS

TRASH-CANNING

Back in fifth grade I (Kurt) wasn't the biggest guy around. Actually, I was one of the shortest guys in my class (and I haven't grown much since). As the school year was wrapping up, my friends and I began talking about what middle school was going to be like. As we talked about this stuff, I found myself getting really nervous. *Am I going to fit in? Am I going to like having seven teachers? Am I going to be able to reach my locker?*

But one of the biggest things I kept asking my little self was, *Am I going to get trash-canned?*

We'd all heard the stories of some poor little sixth grader getting picked up by a group of eighth graders, turned upside down, and dumped into a school trash can. Every time I heard one of these terrifying stories, I'd show a fake smile and give a little nervous giggle, while deep down I was scared to death as I pictured myself facedown in a pile of nasty, smelly, disgusting middle school trash.

On the first day of middle school, as I walked by what seemed like thousands and thousands of trash cans, I remember thinking to myself, *Is this going to be the one? Or maybe that one? Yeah, probably that one because it's really close to my locker. Which big guy is going do it? Him? No, he looks nice. Maybe him, he looks mean. And he's built like a senior in high school. What's it going to feel like? I hope it happens in an empty trash can. Are other people going to see it happen? Will they laugh at me?*

Well, a few days went by, and then a few weeks, and then a few months, and I still hadn't experienced getting tossed into a trash can. In fact, I didn't see *anyone* get trash-canned.

It turned out to be an urban legend—something people talk about that's never really happened. The stories that were told that day in fifth grade were all made up. We'd heard the rumors from our older brothers and sisters, and we just assumed they were true.

So take it from someone who survived middle school—this trash-canning thing is just a bunch of garbage!

CAFETERIA MYSTERY MEAT

What is this stuff? you think to yourself as the cafeteria lady plops a piece of something that looks sorta like some type of meaty substance onto your plate. Your mind instantly takes you to every cartoon, television show, and movie you've ever seen that talks about the dangers of cafeteria mystery meat.

The legend goes something like this: The cafeteria purposely keeps the source of the meat a mystery because they know if students find out what it really is, there will be a major revolt. They disguise the mystery meat in all sorts of ways. They make it into sloppy joes. They blend it into spaghetti sauce. They form it into some sort of loafy shape. The legend is that students are afraid to ask what type of meat it is because they'll be shocked by the answer. Allow us to put an end to this mystery of the mystery meat.

When you stop to think about it, we eat only a few types of meat: chicken, beef, and pork. Just about all the meat you've ever eaten falls into one of those categories. So it makes sense, then, that the mystery meat at school must be chicken, beef, or pork.

Trust us on this one—your cafeteria cook isn't rounding up stray dogs and cats. She's using the usual stuff to make your food. Like all great chefs (your cafeteria cook is a great chef, right?) she probably likes to mix things up from time to time by serving the chicken, beef, or pork in some creative way—some mysterious way!

If you're really worried about what you eat on a daily basis, there are lots more dangerous things than the "mystery meat" at school. Take a second to check out the ingredients label on a package of hot dogs, a can of Red Bull, or a bag of chips. Talk about mysterious!

So the next time the cafeteria lady plops that mysterious meat-like substance on your plate, just close your eyes, open your mouth, and trust that everything will be just fine.

"MY DOG ATE MY HOMEWORK"

Have you ever heard this excuse? C'mon, have you ever *used* this excuse?

Until a few months ago, I (Marko) would have said this is a classic urban legend (a story that gets told as though it's true, but no one knows the real source of it). It's more like the teachers' favorite example of a lame unacceptable excuse. Like, "Now, class, I don't want to hear any excuses about why you don't have your homework done. I won't accept 'I was sick' unless you have a note from a parent. I won't accept 'I was injured' unless you're missing an arm or leg. And I won't accept 'My dog ate my homework' unless you bring in your dog's droppings and prove it to me!"

Or something like that.

But, like I said, that was what I thought until a few months ago. That's when it happened: Our family dog ate my daughter's homework. Seriously. She'd finished her math the night before and set it on the kitchen counter. Then she went to bed. The next morning, Liesl was gathering her stuff for school, and she couldn't find her homework. She asked her mom and me if we'd seen it or moved it, and we all began a search throughout the house for the missing homework.

Finally, we found some little scraps of it near where the dog sleeps. They were just tiny pieces of paper, and one of them had part of a math problem written on it. And get this—we even found a little piece of the math paper still stuck in the dog's hair, just outside his mouth.

Liesl was really bummed, but my wife and I couldn't stop laughing. We wrote a note to Liesl's teacher to explain why her homework wasn't ready to be turned in. The teacher probably thought we were total crazies, absolute nut jobs.

There—this is officially no longer an urban legend. We've provided documented evidence that dogs *can* and *do* eat homework!

THE MYSTERY THAT IS...
THE TEACHERS' LOUNGE

Chances are you've never set foot in the teachers' lounge (sometimes called "the staff room") at your school. Maybe you passed by when the door was open and caught a tiny glance inside. And maybe that glance only furthered your suspicions and raised more questions about what actually goes on in there.

Here are some of the rumors we've heard from middle school kids as to what they believe goes on in the teachers' lounge at their schools:

- "They have free beer in my school's teachers' lounge. The teachers all go in there and get blasted."

- "They have, like, a never-ending pile of doughnuts. There's a secretary whose job it is to make sure the pile of doughnuts never runs out."

- "I heard they have a flat screen TV and a sweet gaming system. The teachers sit in there and play video games, man!"

- "At my school, a kid went into the teachers' lounge and he never came out. No one ever saw him again!"

Yeah. We're sure the teachers' lounge is actually a portal to another planet. And the teachers? They're actually aliens. They come and go, popping back to their home planet to scarf down a hot plate of bleeznots (or whatever they eat) and to pat their six-eyed, four-legged kids on the tops of their three little heads.

The reality of the teachers' lounge is, we're sorry to reveal, boring. We mean WAY boring. Once this is clear, you're gonna *wish* there was an alien portal or at least a never-ending pile o' doughnuts because the truth is *so stinkin' boring!*

The teachers' lounge contains a collection of tables and chairs, as well as a pot of overheated, nasty coffee. Sometimes there's a refrigerator where they keep their little lunches. And there are usually a few motivational posters on the wall that say things like, "Don't kill your students!" (No, we're only kidding.) But that's it. It's just a space for the teachers to get away from their students, do a bit of work, or eat their bologna and mayo sandwiches in peace. Oh, and get a cup of nasty, gut-burner coffee.

Do not live in fear or wonder of the mysterious teachers' lounge. Instead, have pity on its weary inhabitants.

THE POOL ON THE ROOF

Can you imagine a "mystery pool" hidden somewhere on your campus? In a place that only the teachers know about? A pool so wonderful and amazing that they don't allow students to even know it exists? It can't be true, can it?

The urban legends surrounding the mysterious swimming pool come in various forms, but they all revolve around the idea that in just about every middle school across America, there's a hidden swimming pool that only the teachers get to use. Now, for a swimming pool to be hidden so well that students never find it takes some creativity, doesn't it? Never fear, urban legends thrive on creativity. Some of the legends say the pool is actually on the roof and the teachers know of a special staircase leading up to it. Other legends say that in schools with multiple floors, there's actually an entire floor of the building that students don't know about! Supposedly, on this hidden floor there are all kinds of amazing things for the teachers—one of which is the pool.

This urban legend would have to fall under the category of a *conspiracy theory*. A conspiracy theory is when somebody or a group of people believe they are purposely being lied to about some sort of information or a situation. So the idea of a "teachers only" swimming pool hidden somewhere on your campus is a classic conspiracy theory.

Think about it for a second: Why would teachers want to swim together? How many grown-ups do you know who take breaks out of their busy day to swim with their buddies? Also consider the cost. For the price of a swimming pool, your school could get the teachers all kinds of stuff they'd rather have. Most teachers would rather have a fancy new coffeemaker or a hidden stash of paper clips.

So we don't believe this urban legend is true. It just isn't logical. But you don't have to believe us; after all, your teachers could be paying us to protect their secret.

Anyhow, we gotta go. We've been invited to a cool pool party on the roof of some building you know very well.

CAMPUS KINDNESS

MAKING FRIENDS WITH THE NEW KID

STUFF YOU MAY NOT HAVE LEARNED IN MIDDLE SCHOOL: A LITTLE MORE THAN 100 FEET OF HAIR FIBER IS PRODUCED EVERY DAY ON THE AVERAGE ADULT SCALP.

It's a couple months into your seventh-grade year, and you're sitting in homeroom. The teacher stands up and introduces a girl to the rest of the class. "Hey, class, I want you to meet Sarah. This is her first day here at El Rancho. Make sure you say 'hello' to her and make her feel welcome. Her family just moved here from Grand Junction, Colorado."

What are some things you can do to befriend the new kid at your school and help make her new experience a good one?

Introduce yourself. Walk up to her (don't wait for her to come to you), say "hello," and calmly introduce yourself. "Hello, Sarah, my name is _____. Welcome to El Rancho."

Have a conversation. We know this is asking a lot, especially if you're a guy. It requires some people skills and talking a little bit. After you introduce yourself, and if it looks like she wants to talk, begin a conversation by asking her a question or two. Questions like, *What are your favorite things to do? What classes do you have? Do you hate cats?*

Give her a tour. Ask her if you can show her around campus for a few minutes. Show her everything you think she needs to know about—the stinky bathrooms, the cafeteria, the P.E. locker room, the library, the best foods to order at the snack bar, and so on. As you show her around, keep asking her questions and get to know her. Also, as you tour your campus and pass by people you know, make sure you introduce her to them. The more people she meets, the quicker she'll feel connected and known.

Ask her to hang out with you after school. A great way to develop a friendship with the new kid is to hang out off campus. Ask if she wants to come over to your house (make sure you ask your parents first). Or see if your parents (or her parents) will take you to the mall or to your favorite ice cream place.

You don't have to become best friends with the new kid, but it doesn't hurt to be friendly.

USING YOUR GIFTS TO HELP OTHERS

We've heard from a pretty reliable source that you're a gifted individual. The Bible makes it clear that God has given all of us special talents and abilities he hopes we'll use to encourage the people around us.

Ask yourself a few questions: *What do I like? What am I good at? What types of things interest me?* Those are probably pretty easy questions for you to answer, but here's a tougher one: *How can I use my gifts, talents, and abilities to help others in my school?* Here's an even tougher question: *Am I willing to do it?*

God didn't gift you so you'd leave those gifts unopened. He didn't gift you so you'd open the gifts and use them just for yourself. The truth is God gave you your gifts with the expectation that you'll use them to make a difference in the world around you. And it just might be that no place needs you to use your gifts more than your school does.

Are you good at math? Maybe you can tutor someone who's struggling.

Are you a good athlete? What if you decided to ask the kid who always gets picked last to be on your team in P.E.?

Are you good at encouraging others? How about finding the new kid or the loner and inviting him to eat lunch with you?

Do other people look up to you? Think what could happen if you rallied a bunch of your classmates and started a new movement. Like a movement to treat substitute teachers with respect or treat others the way you want to be treated or make the janitor's job easier by picking up your own trash.

What if you started a one-person movement? Like a movement to use your God-given gifts, talents, and abilities to make a difference on your campus.

THE POWER OF YOUR WORDS

Have you ever heard the saying, "Sticks and stones may break my bones but words will never hurt me"? You're probably thinking, Yeah, like 120 times! Well, has anyone told you this saying is a load of junk? It is! The saying should be, "Sticks and stones may break my bones but words can hurt me, too." Actually, words can hurt us even more (emotionally and mentally) and for a longer period of time than any old stick or stone.

The words that come out of your mouth are very powerful. They can either build someone up or tear someone down. They can make someone's day or ruin it. The Bible is very clear about the power of words. (Take a look at James, chapter 3.) By now you probably know how powerful your words are. But if you're like most people, you still have a hard time controlling what comes out of your mouth.

The school environment tests your ability to control your words like no other place can. So what can you do to prevent what comes out of your mouth from causing damage?

Be positive. Be a person who strives to be encouraging to those around you. Have you ever been around someone who's always negative and discouraging? How did it make you feel? It's no fun! It's contagious, like a bad flu. And pretty soon you find yourself being negative, too. Don't be like that person. Look at the positive in every situation, and you'll find that those around you will be more positive, too.

Don't gossip. This might be a tough one for you. Especially when the girls are standing around before class, just chatting up a storm, and one of them says, "Like, ohmigosh, look at her ugly outfit. It's like so 2001. Nasty!" Then another one chimes in with, "And look at her hair. It looks like a bird's nest!" Gossip can be super-damaging. Even if some poor guy never finds out about the things that were said about him, he's getting trashed all the same. So don't jump on the gossip train. Actually, be the person who stops the gossip train from going down the tracks.

Keep it clean! Watch your mouth. Stay strong! Don't use foul language. Be careful about the things you say. When all the guys are sitting around the lunch table telling dirty jokes, don't laugh, don't join in, or better yet, just walk away from the group. There's nothing kind about a dirty mouth.

Your words can be powerful, both in a positive and negative way. As a Christian, one of the biggest ways to damage your reputation as a Christ-follower is to constantly talk in a negative, unkind way.

STICKING UP FOR THE UNDERDOG

When we (Marko and Kurt) were kids, there was a cartoon on TV called *Underdog*. (Actually, as we write this, we've seen previews for a live-action movie about Underdog.)

Underdog was an actual dog. He was a basset hound with big droopy cheeks and long ears who never got mad, never spoke in anything but a quiet monotone voice (yes, he was a talking dog), always spoke in rhyme, and wasn't all that capable of solving the crimes and mysteries that occurred on the show. But he always stumbled onto the solution—eventually.

Underdog's motto was, "Have no fear, Underdog is here!"

Uh, yeah. Do you know what an *underdog* is? No, it's not a dog that's "under" something. An *underdog* is a person (or group of people) not expected to win or succeed. Like, if there are two teams playing against each other in a particular sport and one team is clearly supposed to win, then the other team (the expected losers) is called the "underdog."

The word has a funny origin. It comes from the days when ships were built out of wooden planks. The long trees that were going to be cut into planks were laid across a pit. And these pieces of wood were called "dogs." It took two men to operate the giant saw they used to cut up these big trees, so one guy stood on top of the "dog"—he was called the "overdog"—while the other dude had to stand in the pit and under the plank—making him the "underdog." The underdog would always get covered in sawdust—it was a nasty job!

Anyhow, now that you've had a lesson in word history, we'll get to the point of this chapter. A great way to live out your faith at school is to try to be nice to the guy who's getting sawdust in his face. No, not just in woodshop class. We mean the real-life "underdogs." At your school, the underdog is anyone who's not expected to succeed at whatever—school, gym class, athletics, social settings. It's the loner. It's the kid who struggles to understand a subject. It's the new kid. It's the minority kid. It's the disabled kid. It's the kid with a lisp. It's any kid other kids like to tease.

Jesus *loves* underdogs! We mean, he *REALLY, REALLY* loves them. We DARE you to read one of the gospels (Matthew, Mark, Luke, or John) and find proof that he doesn't. When Jesus says, "Blessed are the meek, for they will inherit the earth" (Matthew 5:5), he's really saying, "Underdogs are my kind of people!"

So stick up for the underdogs at your school. Be nice to the underdogs. Do kind things for the underdogs. Help the underdogs. It's tough when you have sawdust falling in your face all day long!

"DID YOU BRING ENOUGH FOR EVERYBODY?" "WHY, YES, I DID!"

Have you ever had someone give you something cool, like a gift card, and it wasn't even your birthday or a special occasion? How did it make you feel? Surprised? Confused? You may have thought, *Oh no, she wants something from me...or she must have done something wrong and is trying to pay me back.* But to your surprise, you realized she gave it to you just because. How sweet is that?

How much fun would it be if you brought something to school and gave it to someone just because? Or gave it to *everyone* just because? Now, we're not saying everybody in your entire school, but maybe an entire class or your group of friends or everybody on the bus ride home.

One of the best ways to show kindness is by sharing. Here are a few ideas of things you can bring to school and share with everybody:

Bring something for everyone in your lunch crowd. When you sit down for lunch, bust out a bag of candy bars for all your lunch friends. Or bring a huge bag of chips and share with everyone. Or bring an entire case of Capri Sun and give one to everybody.

Bring something for everyone in your class. Bring a couple dozen assorted doughnuts for everybody in your homeroom. Make sure you get permission from your teacher first. Also make sure to get your teacher her favorite doughnut. Or for a class that meets after lunch, bring a tray of brownies for everybody. Make sure you sprinkle some powdered sugar on top of the brownies before you serve them, because that's delicious! Or bring a bag of cookies. Everyone likes a good cookie after lunch.

Bring something healthy for everyone in your P.E. class. Slice up a bunch of juicy oranges, bag them up, and bring them for the class. Or bring a small cooler of ice-cold Gatorade. There's nothing like a cup of Gatorade to rehydrate you after running the mile (the dreaded mile). Don't forget the cups.

Kindness can be shown in a bunch of ways at your school. A fun, surprising way to share kindness is by sharing yummy stuff with everyone, just because.

BIRTHDAY CARDS FOR HOMEROOM

What's one thing everyone in your homeroom has in common? Uh, besides the fact that they're all in the same homeroom. One thing you all have in common is that you were all born. Okay, that's pretty stupid, but here's an idea that's not: Buy a birthday card for every kid in your homeroom. We know it sounds kinda weird, but think about how cool it would be if everybody got one! Everyone likes birthday cards. Yes, everyone. The mean kid who doesn't like anybody or anything? Yep. The guy who hates kittens? Even he likes to get birthday cards. He probably even likes birthday cards with pictures of little kittens on them!

This idea works best if you decide to start right at the beginning of the school year. Tell your homeroom teacher your plan and ask him to get you a list of student birthdays. (Make sure you get your teacher's birthday, too.) Then buy some boxes of cards and spend a couple evenings filling them out. In the top corner of each envelope, lightly write the person's birth date in pencil. Then organize the stack of cards in birth-date order, and set them on your dresser. Or ask your homeroom teacher to keep them in his desk drawer. By doing it this way, you'll get all the work done up front and won't run the risk of forgetting about somebody whose birthday occurs later in the year.

If you're starting later in the school year, simply make up for lost time by handing out belated birthday cards to the people who've already celebrated their birthdays. If a person's birthday falls during a summer month, give her a card sometime in the middle of the school year, like in January or February. Perhaps you could give her a card on her "half birthday" instead.

The fun part about this idea is that you can go about it any way you want. You can either sign the cards with your name or sign them FROM YOUR HOMEROOM. You can hand them out yourself, ask your homeroom teacher to hand them out, or set the card on the birthday person's desk ahead of time. You can make a huge deal out of it or keep it real low-key. You can be known as the giver of cards or you can keep your identity a secret.

Everyone enjoys getting birthday cards.

I WAS A MIDDLE SCHOOL DORK!
—MARKO

When I was in seventh grade, my family moved about a half hour from where I'd lived all my life. The house we moved into didn't have a bedroom for me, but the plan was to build one in the basement—which I thought was the coolest thing in the world.

So for about six months, my "room" was just a corner of the basement (which wasn't very private!). But eventually, my dad and I started putting up the walls. One day while we were hanging the paneling, I asked my dad if we could build a little "secret compartment" into the wall.

I'd always loved secret compartments and passageways. On family trips, we'd been to a few old mansions and castles that had mysterious hiding places and secret stairways and bookshelves that spun around. I remember one place we toured where the boy's room had a secret door built into the wall. Behind the door was a ladder that led to a secret playroom. I thought it was the coolest thing I'd ever seen, and I wanted something secret like that in my new room.

So my dad and I planned a small, secret compartment above the doorframe. We cut out the piece of paneling, put hinges on it, and added a little semi-hidden handle made from a painted nail. Inside, I lined the compartment with a small, plastic box so things wouldn't fall down into the wall. That would be a little *too* secret!

(Oh, let me interrupt myself for a moment. Years later, when I was a young adult and living back at my parents' house for a little while, I was planning to ask my girlfriend, Jeannie, who's now my wife, to marry me. I'd already bought her a diamond ring, so I kept it hidden in my secret compartment for a couple months until the day I proposed.)

Anyway, when the secret compartment was finished, I was so excited. I loved it! It wasn't that big a deal, but I just couldn't contain my excitement. So I did something really, really stupid: I told everyone about my secret compartment. Seriously. Everyone who visited my room, every one of my friends, every family member I showed them all, with beaming pride, my secret compartment.

Small problem—a secret compartment isn't very secret when everyone knows about it. Proof, once again, that I was a middle school dork!

SECTION 10
MISCELLANEOUS
SURVIVAL TIPS

LIFE WITH A LOCKER

Many middle schools today, for a variety of reasons, no longer have lockers, or they just never put them in. As the lockers get older, they can start to look really ugly, they're expensive to maintain, and they can actually be kind of dangerous—someone can slam a hand in the door or slice a finger on a sharp rusty edge. But if your middle school does have lockers, you can consider yourself lucky.

Here are some tips to survive and thrive with a locker in middle school:

Use it. You call this a tip? Well, we've heard many stories about students who have a perfectly functioning locker with a great three-number combination, but they never use it. It sounds crazy, but it's true. The locker is there for your benefit.

- Use it to store your books and folders. Why lug around 23 pounds of books in your backpack if you can store them in your locker?

- Use a hook to hang your Power Rangers lunch bag. A lunch in a backpack only gets smashed and nasty.

- Use the other hook to hang up a light jacket and an umbrella. You never know when the weather is going to change. We understand it can be considered dorky to use an umbrella in middle school. But would you rather be dry and have the nickname "Mary Poppins," or soaking wet and freezing your head off?

Make it your own. It's your locker! Well, not really, but you do get to use it for an entire school year. So personalize it. Put your name in it somewhere. Put up some pictures of your favorite celebrities, your family, and don't forget a picture of that guy you have a crush on. Decorate it for each season of the year. Hang some battery-powered Christmas lights. Put a leprechaun (not a real one) on the door. Hang an Easter basket full of goodies from one of the hooks.

Keep it organized. Keep it clean. Make sure you know where everything is. Sometimes you're in a hurry to get to class, and you have only a minute to grab something from your locker. Don't be late for class because you spent 10 minutes looking for your calculator. Also, a dirty locker can be hazardous to your health and the health of those around you. A peanut butter and jelly sandwich lost in a corner of a locker for three months is not healthy. If you're organized, that sandwich won't have a chance to get lost and all your stuff won't smell like moldy bread.

A locker—a tiny one-foot-by-two-foot space of metal—is a pretty big deal. Make the most of it.

"I LIKE HAVING MY OWN LOCKER!"

—COLTON, 7TH GRADE

CHOOSING WHAT TO WEAR

Have you ever seen someone at school wearing a crazy-looking outfit? One that, no matter how much you looked at it, just didn't look right? You may have been convinced the person got dressed in the dark. Dark green pants, a bright pink button-down shirt with yellow flowers all over it, and, to top it all off, blue socks wrapped in a pair of black shoes.

Okay, maybe you've never seen an outfit that hideous at school. Or you're probably thinking to yourself, *I see that kind of outfit all the time—on my grandpa!* Well, your grandpa can get away with wearing something like that because he's 80 years old! But you'd never be caught wearing something like that to school. Unless, of course, it's "Come Dressed as Your Grandpa Day."

Choosing what to wear is a challenge that's been around for a long time. (To our knowledge, it's been around for *at least* as long as people have been wearing clothes to school.) As you choose what to wear to school, it's important to remember one thing: Just be yourself. Wear what you feel is best for you. We all know this isn't as easy as it sounds, so here are a few things to think about as you choose that next outfit:

Brand names are overrated. We understand that keeping up with the latest fashions is fun (for some). But, this can be super-expensive for your parents, especially if you'll only wear the most popular brand names. Seventy dollars for a pair of jeans is outrageous! It's possible to look good without spending a ton of money. Don't believe us? Just ask your grandpa.

You will be judged by your cover. The reality is people often judge others by what's on the outside—by the clothes they wear. This is totally unfortunate but true. We see many middle schoolers try to fit in with the rich crowd or the Goth crowd or the skater crowd by wearing the latest fashions. Don't let your outsides be controlled by the people you want to hang out with. Be yourself and be confident in who you are.

You do need to watch what you wear. Clothes that are too revealing and immodest give people the wrong impression. Shirts bearing foul language or rude images cause people to assume you're foul and rude, too.

It's important to at least think about what you want to wear or else you'll end up looking like Grandpa. But don't let fashion worries wear you out. (Get it? "Wear" you out? Ha!)

BAD HAIR DAYS

We've all had them. Some of us have had many. Actually, maybe you're reading this chapter because you're having a bad hair day. We want you to know we're here for you, and everything is going to be okay!

You may believe bad hair days only happen to girls, but they can happen to guys, too. But some guys actually make their hair look that way on purpose, and a bad hair day for them is when their hair looks clean and combed.

We want to give you a few survival tips to help with those days when you're saying, "My hair looks terrible! It won't do anything for me!"

Shave it off! Or cut it really short. This idea is for you boys, even though some famous girls have chosen this hairstyle in the past. Actually, bald is Kurt's favorite (and only) hairstyle. It began about 10 years ago. He woke up one morning, and his long brown hair just wasn't flowing or cooperating anymore. So he grabbed the clippers and buzzed it off. He hasn't had a bad hair day since. Actually, he hasn't even had a hair day. The bald look probably isn't for you, but there are lots of cool ways to wear your hair short. And shorter hair is less likely to go bad.

Put it up in a ponytail. Now this tip is primarily for you girls. Some of you longhaired guys can do this, too (if you want to look like a Harley man). The great thing about a ponytail is that it's an easy and quick fix to crazy, out-of-control hair. Make sure you keep a good ponytail clip in your backpack, just in case your hair turns ugly during the school day. If you aren't into ponytails, there are other ways to put your hair up that we don't really know about because we're guys. However, Marko has had long hair lots and lots of times, so he could probably give you some tips.

Try to avoid them. Yes, there *are* ways to avoid the bad hair day:

- Wake up a little earlier so you'll have more time to deal with uncooperative hair.

- Take your shower in the morning. This eliminates bad bed head.

- Use a hair dryer. Girls, you know all about this. Guys, it can work for you, too, so give it a shot!

- Pray! It seems every painting of Jesus shows him with cool-looking, long, wavy, Bible hair. So he just might be able to help you prevent that bad hair day.

Hair is a funny thing and no two heads of hair are alike. You know your hair better than anyone else (we hope). If you try everything and your hair just won't cooperate, remember you can always throw on a hat. Just make sure it's a Los Angeles Angels cap.

THE COMPARISON GAME

"Wow! That one kid in gym class seems to have the sweetest new pair of shoes, like, every month!"

"She is so smart! I'll never be as smart as she is, and it really bugs me."

"Omigosh! He is such a loo-hoo-zer! Just look at those loser clothes and that loser backpack and that loser lunch."

Maybe you've never said any of these things. But you've probably at least *thought* something like them. The comparison game—we all play it. He's got more. She's got less. He's not as cool as I am. She's way cooler than I'll ever be.

People call it the comparison "game" because, like a game, there's no real-life purpose to it. Playing it doesn't benefit anyone, including you. In fact, it's just the opposite—playing the comparison game robs you of life.

Jesus said something very, very cool in John 10:10—"I have come that they may have life, and have it to the full." Part of experiencing that full life Jesus wants us to have is by experiencing *contentment.* Do you know that word? It means to be happy with what you have and who you are.

The Bible makes it clear we shouldn't stand in judgment of other people (see Matthew 7:1-5, for example). This means we shouldn't play the comparison game to identify students who either have less than we do or—in our eyes—*are* less than we are.

The Bible also makes it clear we shouldn't waste our time desiring other people's stuff (see Exodus 20:17, for starters). In this way, we play the comparison game to identify students who have more than we do or—in our eyes—*are* more than we are.

Here's the cold, hard truth: Throughout the rest of your life, no matter who you are, or where you live, or what you do, there will always be—

- People who have more stuff than you do, and people who have less stuff than you do

- People who are cooler than you are, and people who are less cool than you are

- People with more fashion sense than you, and people with less fashion sense than you

- People who are more talented than you are, and people who are less talented than you are

- People who are more popular than you are, and people who are less popular than you are

- People who are luckier than you are, and people who are less lucky than you are

Deal with it! Be happy with who you are and what you have—they're all gifts from God anyhow!

THE POPULARITY PROBLEM

Have you tried holding onto a big handful of water? If you get your hands and fingers interlocked just right, you might be able to accomplish it fairly well, at least for a while. But DUDE! You're leaking! Eventually, the water will leak out and you'll be left holding your hands like an empty bowl.

That's what popularity is like. You try and try and try to hold onto it tightly, but it leaks away. You get a little bit of popularity, but you can't hold onto it. It starts to consume you and take more and more effort and attention. Sooner or later, it becomes the only thing you really care about, which is very, very sad.

Have you ever heard of someone getting mega-rich, only to want even *more* money? Someone asks them, "How much money do you need to be happy?" And they respond, "Just a little bit more." But the wealthier they become, the weirder and weirder they get. They can't trust people anymore, so they withdraw and get lonelier. They spend more time alone, and lose the ability to have normal relationships.

That's what popularity is like. Getting just some of it is never enough. The more you get, the more you want. And the more you get, the harder it is to hold onto. It gets more difficult to trust your friends because it seems like they only want to be with you because you're popular. Eventually, your popularity becomes a curse.

Think about these ideas for a moment:

- It's pretty much impossible to constantly reach for popularity *and* constantly reach for God.

- Only a few teenagers are truly popular just because they're nice. Most popular teenagers are popular because they're willing to use people, step on people, gossip, lie, and be mean. Is that who you want to be?

- God digs the unpopular. Really. Of course, God loves everyone. But God seems to have a very special place in his heart for the unnoticed, the losers, the forgotten, the hurting, and the mistreated.

THREE FINAL THOUGHTS FROM MARKO

Oh, man! Kurt and I agreed to wrap up this book with three final tips from each of us. But after giving you 73 other bits of advice, it's really hard to pick just three as my "final thoughts." But here we go...

Enjoy the ride! Middle school is a wild ride, baby! And no matter what kind of school you're in (or aren't in), these years in your life—from 11 to 14—are all about change, transition, weirdness, the unknown, confusion, lightning bolts of insight, growth, doubt, understanding, and joy. And I could list 100 more words. Middle school isn't easy. In fact, it's really difficult! Kurt and I know that, and we're praying for you. But you'll have a *much* better—I mean, way, way, *way* better—time in middle school if you choose to loosen up and enjoy the ride.

Have you ever ridden a horse? When a horse gets going, it moves through a speed called "trotting." It's just a bit faster than walking, but slower than a run. It's wildly bumpy. If you're riding a horse that's trotting and you tighten up all your muscles and make your back rigid, you'll get slammed. It hurts like crazy. You might even get knocked off the horse. But if you loosen up and bounce along with the bumps, it's a fun ride. I suggest you approach middle school the same way.

Explore, explore, and explore some more! As you get older—even in high school—you'll start to narrow down your interests and friendships and how you spend your time. But now isn't the time to do that. Try new things. Explore with your mind. Make new friends of all different kinds. Of course, I'm not suggesting you "explore" in a way that would be displeasing to God or harmful to you. (In other words, I'm not saying, "Hey! Try drugs, try murder, try everything!") But these middle school years are perfectly suited for you to try new things and to begin the task of discovering who you are and who God made you to be.

Look for Jesus! Jesus isn't playing hide-and-seek with you. But we still have to look for him if we want to spend time with him. And once you start looking for Jesus, you'll be surprised by all the places you find him—in the lives of other people, in history, in the beautiful logic of a math theory or physics lesson, in your own mind and imagination, in your family, and in nature (to name just a few). And, of course, you'll also find Jesus in the Bible. The more time you spend with Jesus, the more he'll transform your life. So practice watching for him!

THREE FINAL THOUGHTS FROM KURT

It was hard to decide what my three "final thoughts" would be. This book is full of ideas, but there's still so much we could talk about for surviving life at school.

But if I only get to share three biggies, then they'd have to be—

Be more in love with Jesus than with anything else. Love Jesus more than you love the idea of being popular. Love Jesus more than you love the idea of being liked by that cute boy or girl. Love Jesus more than you love getting good grades. Love Jesus more than you love being accepted and fitting in. One of my favorite verses in the Bible is Matthew 6:33—"But seek first his kingdom and his righteousness, and all these things will be given to you as well." It reminds us to keep Jesus first in our lives.

Show some fruit! The Bible points out some of the things that should be visible signs that we're God's kids—that his spirit is alive in us. It calls these qualities "the fruit of the Spirit." They're listed in Galatians 5:22-23. Take a look: "But the fruit of the Spirit is love, joy, peace, patience, kindness, goodness, faithfulness, gentleness and self-control." How could your day-to-day school experience be different if you allowed these things to show up in your life? Try it; I think you'll like it!

Don't give up! I sure wish reading this little book guaranteed an easy middle school experience for you, but it doesn't. I wish I could promise that if you stay in love with Jesus and model the fruit of the Spirit you won't have any bad days, but that would be a lie. The truth is that middle school is a crazy journey full of ups and downs, highs and lows, good days and bad days. But hang in there! Don't give up! Trust Jesus, surround yourself with supportive friends, and ask your parents for help when you need it. You'll make it!

"SMILE...LIFE GOES ON!!"

—REBECCA, 7TH GRADE

LISTEN TO WHAT JESUS HAS TO SAY TO YOU. IN THIS 60-DAY DEVO YOU'LL RECEIVE DAILY LETTERS FROM JESUS AND SPEND SOME TIME JOURNALING YOUR THOUGHTS BACK TO HIM AS YOU TAKE PART IN THE CONVERSATION.

Conversations with Jesus
Getting in on God's Story
Youth for Christ

RETAIL $10.99
ISBN 0-310-27346-3

Visit **www.invertbooks.com** or your local bookstore.

MOST TEENAGERS THINK THAT BEING A CHRISTIAN MEANS DOING
THE RIGHT THING. BUT FIGURING OUT WHAT THE "RIGHT THING"
IS CAN BE A CHALLENGE. IT'S DIFFICULT FOR STUDENTS TO TELL
THE DIFFERENCE BETWEEN GOD'S PLAN FOR THEM AND WHAT
OTHER CHRISTIANS SAY IS GOD'S PLAN FOR THEM. AUTHOR MARK
MATLOCK WILL GUIDE YOUR STUDENTS THROUGH GOD'S WORD TO
HELP THEM FIGURE OUT WHAT GOD REALLY WANTS FROM THEM.

What Does God Want from Me?
Understanding God's Desire for Your Life
Mark Matlock
RETAIL $9.99
ISBN 0-310-25815-4

EVEN IN THE DARKEST HOUR, GOD KEEPS SHINING HIS LIGHT INTO OUR LIVES. TRUE VOL. 1 IS A COLLECTION OF STORIES FROM STUDENTS, ROCK STARS, AND OTHERS ABOUT WHAT HAPPENS WHEN GOD STEPS INTO THE MESS OF LIFE. IF YOU'RE STRUGGLING WITH DOUBT, PAIN, OR TROUBLING CIRCUMSTANCES, GRAB THIS BOOK. IT'LL HELP YOU DISCOVER WHAT'S TRUE.

True Vol. 1
Real Stories about God Showing Up
in the Lives of Teens
Irene Dunlap

RETAIL $12.99
ISBN 0-310-25268-7

INSIDE THE PAGES OF THIS BOOK, STUDENTS WILL FIND TRUE STORIES BY TEENAGERS AND YOUNG ADULTS ABOUT PAIN, LOSS, LIFE, AND GROWING UP. READERS WILL GET GLIMPSES OF GOD WHEN THEY READ ABOUT WHAT HAPPENED WHEN GOD STEPPED IN DURING DESPERATE STRUGGLES AND SOUL-SEARCHING MOMENTS. AS STUDENTS EXPERIENCE THESE STORIES, THEY'LL LEARN NEW THINGS ABOUT GOD AND THEMSELVES.

True Vol. 2
52 Stories about God Showing Up
in the Every Day
Irene Dunlap

RETAIL $12.99
ISBN 0-310-25302-0

Visit **www.invertbooks.com** or your local bookstore.

LOSERS CLUB
LESSONS FROM THE LEAST LIKELY
HEROES OF THE BIBLE

invert

"Jeff has knocked it out of the park with *Losers Club*. This is a book to get us in touch with
the mind of God, who always looks past the outward appearances and into the heart."
–Chris Tomlin

JEFF KINLEY

LOSER'S CLUB IS A REAL-LIFE LOOK AT BIBLE CHARACTERS
SUCH AS MOSES, SOLOMON, DAVID, THOMAS, RAHAB, AND
OTHERS. EACH VIGNETTE REVEALS PEOPLE WHO STRUGGLE
WITH WEAK FAITH, CONFUSION, AND FRUSTRATION. THESE
STORIES WILL HELP STUDENTS CONNECT WITH THESE
FLAWED HEROES, FIND ENCOURAGEMENT IN THEIR
STORIES, AND GET INSPIRED BY GOD'S LOVE AND CARE FOR
"LOSERS."

The Losers Club
Lessons from the Least Likely Heroes of the Bible
Jeff Kinley
RETAIL $9.99
ISBN 0-310-26262-3

invert

Visit **www.invertbooks.com** or your local bookstore.